Angels to Bear You Up

MW00658979

OTHER BOOKS AND AUDIO BOOKS

BY JUDY C. OLSEN:

Beyond the Horizon

Angels Round About: True Stories of the Lord's Tender Mercies

Angels TO BEAR YOU UP

True Stories of the Lord's Tender Mercies

JUDY C. OLSEN

Covenant Communications, Inc.

Covenant

Cover image: *Colorful Butterfly Sitting on Flower* © Pawel Gaul, courtesy of iStockphotography.com

Cover design copyright © 2012 by Covenant Communications, Inc.

Published by Covenant Communications, Inc.
American Fork, Utah

Copyright © 2012 by Judy C. Olsen
All rights reserved. No part of this book may be reproduced in any format or in any medium without the written permission of the publisher, Covenant Communications, Inc., P.O. Box 416, American Fork, UT 84003. This work is not an official publication of The Church of Jesus Christ of Latter-day Saints. The views expressed within this work are the sole responsibility of the author and do not necessarily reflect the position of The Church of Jesus Christ of Latter-day Saints, Covenant Communications, Inc., or any other entity. The Church does not endorse this book.

Printed in the United States of America
First Printing: January 2012

18 17 16 15 14 13 12   10 9 8 7 6 5 4 3 2 1

ISBN-13: 978-1-60861-571-1

To my sisters: Patricia Thelin, Gloria Martinez,
Carol Stewart, and Sara Hacken, who have been friends
and supporters throughout my life. Thank you for your great
examples and for living your lives through faith and good works.

Acknowledgments

First and foremost, I wish to acknowledge the hand of the Lord in collecting these stories. Gathering them has truly been a story in itself, so I must believe that somewhere in these pages there are special messages meant to touch the heart and soul of someone out there.

I want to thank all those who have contributed to this work. They have shared some choice spiritual experiences and allowed us a moment's glimpse into their hearts. Such stories strengthen, uplift, and teach us that Someone wiser than we are is always nearby and that angels do indeed watch over us.

Introduction

A comment Brigham Young made, which I included in the introduction to volume 1, bears repeating here. He stated: "There is no doubt, if a person lives according to the revelations given to God's people, he may have the Spirit of the Lord to signify to him his will, and to guide and to direct him in the discharge of his duties, in his temporal as well as his spiritual exercises. I am satisfied, however, that in this respect, we live far beneath our privileges" (Brigham Young, from *Discourses of Brigham Young,* selected and arranged by John A. Widtsoe, 1943, 32).

What are our privileges? I believe that as we listen to the personal testimony of faithful Latter-day Saints, we begin to glimpse what Brigham Young knew about our ability to receive guidance from the Spirit. All of us would like to live up to our privilege of obtaining help, guidance, and answers to prayer. Is there a way to better understand just how great a privilege we have been given?

Perhaps we can gain a better appreciation of our potential as we read about others who keep the commandments, pray, and receive help, protection, comfort, guidance, and inspiration through the challenges of life. To this end, the stories in this book offer to all who read them some small idea of the great spiritual blessings that await the faithful.

—Judy C. Olsen

Table of Contents

How Excellent Is Thy Lovingkindness, O God!

—Psalms 36:7

And he shall turn the heart of the fathers to the children, and the heart of the children to their fathers.

—Malachi 4:6

Snatched from the Jaws of Death

By Bill Willson

My father left our family when I was only five years old. He was an alcoholic, but I didn't know that until later. He received a court order to leave his family until he was free of the addiction. From that time on, I had a secret fantasy that Dad would one day come back—that he would be there for me.

So when Mom and I learned of my father's death on skid row in Seattle, Washington, due to acute alcoholism, this secret fantasy long stored in my then eleven-year-old heart died with him. Much to our surprise, he had a note and a bank book in his pocket. The note named me his sole heir. The bank account had more than three thousand dollars in it. In recalling this as an adult, I realized that while he was away from us for six years, all his thoughts and efforts were focused on me and that he had sacrificed much to save that money for me.

One of my fondest, most precious little-boy memories is of my father taking me fishing in my big red Radio Flyer wagon. We lived in an alley off University Avenue, not far from the San Francisco Bay. Dad loved to fish, and he took me often.

Shortly after my father's death, I began to fish every chance I got. One day when I was thirteen, I grabbed my fishing gear and jumped on my bike. I headed for two barges tied up behind the Bay Meadows Racetrack. The bay was as smooth as glass, the sun felt warm on my face and arms, and it was a good day to go fishing. In no time at all, I had my first fish, a fairly large Jack Smelt. I attached the fish to my stringer, a rope with wire clips that I used to hang my catch back in the water while I continued to fish. Because the stringer wasn't quite long enough to reach the water from the top of the deck, I lay down on the edge of the barge with my head and shoulders over the edge to attach the stringer to a cleat about a foot and a half below the main decking.

Once the stringer was in place, I baited my hook again and tossed it over the side. I had barely settled into a rhythm again when I caught my second Jack Smelt. This one was bigger than the first, and I was excited to be having such a great fishing day.

Too bad there isn't anyone here to share the day with, I thought. I laid down on the edge of the barge, and after attaching the fish to the stringer, I began lowering it into the water. Just then, a small ground swell from a passing ferryboat far out in the bay came in, and the barges slowly rose up and yawed apart as the ripple passed between them. I was intent on my task and oblivious to the danger of the two barges that were about to come crashing back together with enough force to grind my puny little body into jelly.

Suddenly, from out of nowhere, a powerful force seized me and jerked me off the deck, literally snatching me out of the jaws of death. As this power calmly set me on my feet, I looked up into the eyes of a gentle, old man. He spoke kindly to me. "You ought to be more careful, son. The world is a dangerous place. Your life is precious."

I was shaking because the last thing I remembered seeing, just before looking into those eyes, was the two barges crunching together just inches from my head. I turned to look back at the fateful spot. When I returned my gaze to where the old gentleman had stood, he was gone. He had simply vanished. There was no place for him to go because the barges were flat and there were no solid structures above deck. They were moored at the edge of a forty-to-fifty-acre, flat, empty parking area next to the racetrack. I couldn't see anyone around.

Over the years, I have often thought back on that event. I was not a member of the Church then, and I didn't know what to think. In my fright, I didn't get a very good look at the man, but I'll never forget those blue-gray eyes looking down at me while he explained how fragile mortality is. I had seen those same eyes looking at me when I was a little boy, when my father had lived with us. And I continue to see them looking back at me every time I look in the mirror.

When I was seventeen, I joined the Church, but I didn't become deeply converted until I was twenty-five. Then decades passed. Although I have never again actually seen the man who rescued me,

I have sometimes felt someone has been there for me at times when I have needed help. During my years in the navy and later when I worked in construction, I sometimes experienced danger. I remember several times when I had close calls with life-threatening circumstances, but no harm came to me.

After many years, I began doing family history work, and the day came when I went to the temple to do the work for my father. I have often wondered if one reason I had been saved that day on the deck was so I could do the work that brought saving ordinances to him and other family members.

My childhood secret fantasy that my dad would one day come back—that he would be there for me—has now come full circle. In my heart, I believe we have been there for each other. I know he saved my life that day. And I also feel that, in a very special way, I have helped save his.

Bill Willson was born and raised in the East Bay area of San Francisco, California. As an active member of the League of Utah Writers, his genre preference is as eclectic as is his taste in literature. After Bill retired from a career in land engineering, he obtained a degree in English from Utah State University. When his wife, Marjorie, retired, the couple served a two-year proselytizing mission to Mexico City, Mexico. The Willsons have seven children, twenty grandchildren, and two great-grandchildren.

Did I not speak peace to your mind concerning the matter? What greater witness can you have than from God?

—D&C 6:23

He Didn't Understand

By L. C. Liadan

Right after I graduated from the University of Utah in nursing, I found a job in the postsurgical intensive care unit at Primary Children's Hospital in Salt Lake City. While I was working the afternoon shift (three to eleven p.m.), an eight-year-old boy came into our unit after spending several hours in surgery. He was born with several birth defects, and during this surgery, the doctors had worked on some of his heart deficiencies.

He came into the unit at about three p.m., and I was assigned as his nurse. Nursing care on post-surgical heart patients is very intensive. The small patient had tubes everywhere so we could monitor his heart, lungs, and oxygen levels in the blood. He couldn't talk because of the tube that had been inserted into his lungs, and he was sedated with medications to decrease the load on his heart. His parents came in every hour, as permitted, to check on him. Each time, I would give his parents updates on his condition.

Everything seemed to be going well when I ended my shift. I was scheduled to be back at seven a.m. the next day (they call that a short change), so when I returned, I was reassigned to this young boy. His recovery seemed to be going smoothly until about noon. All of a sudden, his heart stopped. We started resuscitation immediately. Unfortunately, his heart could not take the added stress, and he passed away.

It was a tough time for the parents. After I cleaned the body, I spent some time with the parents so they could grieve the loss of their son. It was an emotional day for all of us.

When I went home that afternoon, I was exhausted and wasn't in the best mood. My brother, his wife, and their children were visiting my parents. I tried to socialize, but with the thought of this young boy's death still vivid in my mind, I found it difficult. Soon my father turned to me and said, "If you can't handle being a nurse, maybe you should find another occupation you would enjoy more."

I froze. I had said nothing to my family of my experiences throughout the last forty-eight hours or of the loss of one of my patients, and his criticism touched a nerve. I felt a flash of anger and yelled, "How dare you judge me. You don't know what kind of nurse I am or what it's like being a nurse."

The moment the words left my mouth, I regretted yelling at my father. I left the room and rushed to my bedroom. I threw myself on my bed, feeling hurt, exhausted, and frustrated, all the while still grieving the loss of my patient. As tears streamed down my cheeks, I prayed in my mind, *Father, why is my father so insensitive?*

Immediately, I felt a warmth forming at the top of my head and flowing down my body. It felt as if someone had placed his hands on my head. As the warmth flowed throughout my being, I felt at peace. Then I heard a quiet voice in my mind say, *Forgive him, for he does not understand.*

Never before had I experienced such a powerful spirit enter into my soul. This experience taught me that not only does God care about me, but He also cares about that little boy, my father, and anyone else who judges without cause and speaks without knowing.

L.C. Liandan lives in the Midwest. She has been a nurse for more than thirty-five years. Presently, she travels throughout the country teaching employees and employers how to be safe in the workplace. She also loves to write and read in her spare time.

For I am persuaded, that neither death, nor life,
nor angels, nor principalities, nor powers, nor things
present, nor things to come,

Nor height, nor depth, nor any other creature, shall be
able to separate us from the love of God, which is
in Christ Jesus our Lord.

—Romans 8:38–39

Three Short Days of Life

By Amy Maddocks

A few years ago, my son died after only three short days on this earth. My daughter had been born seventeen years previously, and I had waited those many long years to have another child—even after many doctors had told me I couldn't have more children. I adored my stepdaughters who lived with us for part of the year, but I always longed for another child. Then, at long last, I finally had my little boy—only to have him suddenly taken from me. It seemed more than my heart could stand. For months after his death, I struggled with my beliefs; in my broken mind, I blamed my Father in Heaven for taking Connor away from me so soon.

A few days after Connor died, the bishop came to our house and counseled me. His words were meant to calm and soothe my troubled soul, but instead they made me more angry than I thought possible. He told me I would know soon what Connor's purpose here on Earth was, and he explained that even though life seemed bleak and dreary at that moment, in time I would come to understand why this had happened. He also told me to be very proud of myself because I was chosen to be the mother of a very special angel—one that I would have the chance to raise at another time—but he was needed now in the spirit world more than he was needed on earth.

I listened to his words, spoken with such sincerity and kindness. I nodded at the appropriate times, responded when I thought necessary, and said good-bye soon after. Shutting the door behind him, I plopped myself onto the couch, curled my legs underneath me, rested my chin on my knees, and tried to focus on his words. Looking around the room made that hard to do. Only the curio light was on, so the room had a glow about it like candlelight.

Flowers and plants from well-wishers covered every surface in the room. On the table in the corner, nestled next to the sewing machine, were layers of beautiful blue and white silk, like soft clouds. I would take these clouds and form them, by hand, into my son's final resting clothes. Cards lay scattered about, dishes from neighbors overflowed the sink, and the smell of fresh laundry done by hands other than mine wafted up the stairs. It seemed as though my entire house had been transformed, in this short time, to reflect death, where just days before it had been full of life and vitality.

How can I find answers in all this misery? I thought angrily to myself. Nothing in my entire life had prepared me for such a tragedy. What made my bishop think I would find good in this? I turned away from his words and crawled into my bed like I was crawling into a shell. Here, I would spend a good portion of my time away from the world, trying to make sense of the senseless.

The next few months were torturous, but only because I made them so. I would spend hours trying to console myself without once getting on my knees and praying to the only One who could understand me the most. My husband and mother begged and pleaded with me to take my problems to the Lord, but nothing anybody said to me would change my mind. I was resolute that my son had died because I had failed somehow, and the Lord had allowed it.

One dark day, I heard my cell phone beep, alerting me to a text message. It was from my husband. He explained to me in length that he felt Connor was in heaven and that perhaps our son was disappointed that his mother kept blaming herself and God for his death. Then my husband posed a question: how was Connor supposed to do the work he needed to do if he was always concerned and worried about his mournful mother? He suggested I focus on what Connor needed from me—to be his mom and do what was best for him. I thought about that. *To be Connor's mom.* To do what was best for him. I realized it was time for me to forgive myself and ask the Lord for guidance.

As I sat on the edge of my bed and read the words, the blinds drawn, making my room at midday look like nighttime, tears pooled in my eyes and slowly dropped onto my cell phone. I knew in my heart and soul that my husband was right. The Lord had prompted him to deliver that message to me. I had never even considered the fact that I might be holding Connor back from what he had to do. I had to move on.

So I walked around to the side of my bed, knelt down as I had so many times before—but had not done for months—and poured my heart out to the Lord. I don't know how long I was there or what exactly transpired between me and my Heavenly Father that day, but I arose much later a changed person. There is strength in submission, and I had given up my fears and negativity only to be showered with peace and contentment.

As I walked out of my dark bedroom and down my dim hallway, it was as if I were traveling through a foggy tunnel that had a bright gladness waiting for me at the end. I came out into my front room with renewed strength to face my problems. As I looked around, I saw what was truly there: a bright, cheerful home with beautiful plants to remember my son by, molds of his hands and feet displayed lovingly, and pictures celebrating Connor's time with us on earth. No longer did I see doom and despair. No longer did I see my mistakes and failures. I saw bliss. I was the mother of an angel; something I could and should be proud of.

Comfort had come to me in the form of technology—my dear husband and his cell phone. That one text message changed my entire life. It reached me in my darkness and isolation, where I had not yet let anyone or anything in. I could have wallowed in my misery for an eternity, but instead, because my husband had not given up trying and because he had reached out to me in every way possible, he finally succeeded with a text message!

My life turned into something more beautiful and fulfilling than I had ever thought possible. The blessings of healing I received from that one moment were a direct result of the influence of the Lord. It was as if the Lord was speaking to me, letting me know I could only get through this tragedy if I turned my worries over to Him instead of the world.

I started looking for opportunities to serve others. In fact, I felt a strong pull toward anyone who needed assistance. I joined support groups for families who had lost children. I pulled our extended family together, and we did service projects around the community. We joined the March of Dimes, later to become the ambassador family, hoping the money we raised would help prevent another family from having to experience what we had. We started "kindness" projects, spreading random acts of kindness and helping to pay it forward (we have members in our cause as far away as Florida). I now give presentations on my story and how we can all change the world—doing one small act of kindness daily.

All this service is in memory and honor of my son. None of this would have happened had we not gone through this trial. Hundreds of lives have been changed and improved because of the life and loss of Connor—and because my husband was willing to listen to the Lord and deliver the message only He could give.

Life has changed in many ways since my son died, but we have made those changes positive ones. I am now able to believe in my bishop's counsel, and I have faith in his words. It took me a long time—some would say too long—to come to that conclusion, but I have come to it nonetheless. I don't waste any of my time on "what-ifs" anymore. I focus on the positive. And I focus on the fact that I am surrounded by wonderful people: my husband, my bishop, and all the people in my life who mean so much to me and never gave up on me.

Even though I can no longer have more children, I am extremely grateful to have my daughter and wonderful stepchildren who bless my life. The Lord sent these special souls to me, and they lifted me up and supported me when I needed it the most. They, too, suffered the loss of their brother, but they join with me in celebrating the amazing things in our lives that happen on a daily basis because of the three short days Connor spent with us. I will be forever grateful for my trials because they make me the person I am today—the proud mother of angels, some who walk and one who soars.

Amy Maddocks lives in the beautiful mountain valley of Cache County, Utah, with her husband and children. She is very active in her community as a volunteer and is currently in the Young Women presidency of her ward. She graduated from Utah State University with a degree in education and currently teaches middle school. You can learn more about Connor's story and Amy on her website: www.amymaddocks.com

And I was led by the Spirit, not knowing beforehand the things which I should do.

—1 Nephi 4:6

They Took Me In

By Patricia Ward

I have never believed in coincidence, even before I joined the Church.

At age fifteen, I tried to commit suicide. I got scared after swallowing about half a bottle of Tylenol and spent several hours at the local hospital dealing with the results of taking Ipecac syrup to make me throw up.

During the summer of that same year, my family, except for my stepfather, who stayed behind to work, camped at our usual location north of Peterborough, Ontario, Canada. We planned to stay several weeks, which was a relief, in some ways, from the dreadful life I had to endure with my stepfather at home.

There were a number of other families camping in the area, and a few weeks before my sixteenth birthday, I met and befriended a young man named Jay. We spent a lot of time together. As the days passed pleasantly, he began to notice a marked change in my behavior on the weekends when my stepfather came up to the campsite as opposed to the rest of the week, when he was absent.

As Jay and I became better acquainted, I gave him a brief sketch of what my home was like: my stepfather liked to drink, and when he did, he became very abusive to me—although he did not treat his own children the same way. Later, Jay asked me to talk to his parents. His concern both surprised and touched me greatly. So I spent time getting to know his parents and explaining to them some of the things I was dealing with.

To my surprise, his parents made a wonderful offer: if things ever became more difficult than I could handle, I could call them—collect—and they would come get me. Soon after, they left for home. I was sorry to see them go.

The weekend of my sixteenth birthday, Jay rode his bike all the way back to the campground to spend just one night with us then returned home the next day.

My stepfather arrived to spend his two-week vacation with us soon after Jay left, and my heart sank. He was already drunk when he arrived, and he continued drinking into the night. An intolerable situation rapidly became incredibly worse. The name-calling and hitting were bad enough when he was sober but so much worse when he was drunk, and I had nowhere to go to get away from him. He had brought a considerable amount of beer with him, so I knew from experience that things would not get better.

The previous year, for example, I had sat on a picnic table in an unused site for several hours during a thunderstorm, even though I am terrified of storms, until my mother informed me that my stepfather had passed out and I was safe for a while. Sitting in a raging storm was better than being near *him*—that's how bad it was. This year was no different. I did all I could to avoid him. His rages were so terrifying that I was constantly afraid for my life.

The offer Jay's family made stayed ever present in my mind. Because they lived so far away, I hesitated. But after a week of living in terror, I was desperate. It was hard to stay out of my stepfather's sight all the time, and I hated living in fear hour after hour. The kind offer of help from Jay's family finally became a beacon of hope I could not ignore. I knew what I had to do. I slipped away to make the call from the pay phone by the camp store.

On the following Sunday, in the early hours of dawn, I walked away from the campsite with my small case of possessions, leaving a message with my sister that I had gone to Toronto. My sister, whom I had awakened, forgot to mention anything to my mother until after the local police had been called. After hearing my sister's explanation, the police told my mother there was nothing they could do, as I was of legal age, which at that time in Canada was sixteen.

I talked to my mother the next day, however, and let her know I was safe. I assured her that if I had any trouble, I would let her know. I believe Mother was greatly relieved that I had found a way to get out.

When I moved in with Jay's family, I marveled that a family—strangers, really—would take the time to retrieve a teenage girl they knew little about, other than that she was suffering. I knew next to nothing about them—only that they had offered sorely needed refuge.

They took me into their home, and Jay moved in with his brother in order to give me my own room. His parents even redecorated Jay's room for me, which touched my heart deeply. I enrolled at the local high school.

I soon found out this family belonged to a church I was not familiar with: The Church of Jesus Christ of Latter-day Saints. They invited me to attend church with them my first Sunday there, and I agreed. Missionaries were visiting their eight-year-old daughter, who was preparing for baptism, and she invited me to join their discussions. I began listening and asking questions.

Three months after moving in with this family, I was baptized. My baptism marked the beginning of a new life for me. This wonderful family assisted me in applying for student welfare, a Canadian benefit for which I qualified, and helped me find my own place to live. Even though I spent only three months with them, they set my feet on a new path. For the first time in my life I was safe, I was living on my own, and I was progressing toward meaningful goals. Jay's family checked on me often, and I was thankful to live in peace at last. I finished high school, something that might not have happened if I had not walked away from the campsite that day.

I kept in touch with my mother and visited my family at Easter and Christmas. Mother was deeply grateful for the wonderful new opportunities that had come into my life.

I have always thought that Jay's family may well have saved my life. They certainly gave me a home where I was safe, they gave me the gospel, and they steered me toward a healing future. Now, with years to reflect on what happened, I am struck by the fact that even before I knew about the Church, the Lord was aware of my dreadful situation and opened doors not only to safety but also to faith, hope, and a loving family. I often think of Jay's family as angels sent to help a foundering soul.

Patricia Ward lives in Alberta, Canada, with her husband and daughter.

I do know that whosoever shall put their trust in God
shall be supported in their trials, and their
troubles, and their afflictions.

—Alma 36:3

Would He Live?

By Kelly Clark

I was fortunate to be part of a large extended family scattered throughout Utah. JoDee and Ryan Stott, part of that family, lived only five minutes away. Around noon on July 24, 2010, I received one of those phone calls we all dread. It was JoDee's brother calling to tell me Ryan had just been involved in a serious car accident and that no one yet knew if he would live. He explained that JoDee was on her way to the trauma center in Salt Lake City and asked if I would go down to be with her until the rest of the family, most of whom were driving up from St. George, Utah, could get there.

I immediately drove the thirty or so miles to downtown Salt Lake City and found JoDee with Ryan's father in the waiting room at the hospital. Ryan was in surgery. As we waited to hear from the doctors, JoDee explained what had happened that morning.

Ryan, who works a night shift for a company in Centerville, was on his way home when he drove onto Highway 89 heading north. He had just talked to JoDee on his cell phone to let her know he was on his way when he came upon a double-trailer diesel truck going slowly in his lane as it struggled up an incline. Since Ryan was going highway speed, those involved in the investigation theorized that he looked over his shoulder to change lanes, but in that instant, he came up behind the truck too fast and slammed into the back of it.

A highway patrolman happened to be just minutes behind Ryan and came onto the scene of the wreck before it had even been called in. Because of the severity of Ryan's injuries and the internal bleeding, life flight was called, and Ryan was transported quickly to the trauma center in Salt Lake. This rapid response gave Ryan a chance.

This same highway patrolman also just happened to be JoDee and Ryan's neighbor and immediately recognized Ryan. The patrolman called Ryan's father, who lived near JoDee, and told him what had happened. He suggested he quickly get JoDee to the hospital but to do it without panicking her. He was not sure if Ryan would live, but he wanted JoDee to be there in either case. Word quickly spread throughout the family, and that was when I received the phone call.

JoDee's father-in-law, in his wisdom, took another route to Salt Lake to avoid the scene of the accident, where they were still cleaning up the wrecked vehicles. The pictures on the news and Internet were gruesome, and for several weeks after the accident, we couldn't drive by that spot without experiencing a rush of emotion. It was a blessing for all of us not to have seen the mangled car that morning.

Because of the immediate call from the highway patrolman, JoDee and her father-in-law arrived at the hospital only minutes after Ryan arrived by life flight. Soon after, Ryan's cousin arrived. Normally, the patient is rushed right into surgery, but because of the seriousness of his injuries and the belief that he would not survive, the hospital officials respected Ryan's religion and allowed family members to administer a blessing to him. A small miracle!

The purpose of this first surgery was to find the source of the internal bleeding and stop it. As we waited in the waiting room for news from the doctor, I asked JoDee how understanding her boss would be if she needed to take time off to be with Ryan for the next several days. Ironically, her job had just ended, and she told me she wouldn't be starting her new job for a week or two, so she was available to spend all the time she needed at the hospital with Ryan. In addition, because JoDee was changing jobs, just a few weeks before, the family had decided to change over their insurance coverage from her workplace to Ryan's. At the time they completed the paperwork, Ryan had decided to go ahead and enroll the family in full coverage on a much better plan than they'd previously had. More small blessings.

Another small miracle occurred when Ryan had left for work that night and had not been able to find the keys to their smaller car. He had been forced to drive their Jeep to work. The Jeep was a taller, sturdier vehicle than the one he normally drove, which prevented the car from sliding under the truck upon impact and provided a little more protection to Ryan. If he had been driving the smaller car, his chances of dying on impact would have been much greater. Despite this, the Jeep did not have air bags, and Ryan had not been wearing his seat belt, so he sustained many serious injuries.

The doctor approached us in the waiting room and informed us that he had been able to find the source of the internal bleeding. It appeared that upon impact, the steering wheel had cut into Ryan's stomach and sliced his pancreas in half. In order to stop the bleeding, they had to remove all of his spleen and most of his pancreas. As the pancreas is an organ that is necessary to sustain life, they removed only enough of it to stop the bleeding and left just enough that he would live.

At this point, although Ryan was in critical condition, he was now stable. We had hope. The next step was to do an MRI to determine if there was significant damage or bleeding on the brain. The results showed no significant brain injury. Another miracle, and another seed of hope! After this, we were all allowed to see Ryan. We gathered around his bed as he lay still and unmoving. JoDee stood next to him and held on to his hand. We took turns talking to him, but as JoDee spoke, she felt his fingers move inside her hand. He could hear her and respond!

Ryan was once more taken into surgery, this time to repair the damage to his legs and knees. He had a broken femur, and they placed a rod in his leg. One kneecap was dislocated and the other one crushed. Doctors repaired both with a number of pins and staples, and Ryan was blessed not to have further surgeries to replace his kneecaps.

Many family members and friends stopped by the hospital that day to offer JoDee love and support. Priesthood holders administered additional blessings to Ryan to help him heal and to reduce the pain. People brought cards, food, love, and comfort.

The following day the doctors began to ease Ryan out of a medically induced coma, and the road to recovery began. JoDee and Ryan live in a small community between Layton and Ogden. Word spread quickly, and JoDee's neighbors rallied around her and her family to provide support. The day after the accident, many people fasted for Ryan, and even more offered constant prayers for him and his family. Ryan's name was put on the prayer roll at the temple.

A couple days after the accident, JoDee stopped at a nearby gas station to fill up her car. She went inside to prepay for the gas, and the clerk told JoDee to go ahead and fill her tank. Upon her confused look—she was only planning on putting in a few dollars' worth of gas—the clerk explained that the community had started leaving donations for her at the gas station so she would have enough gas money to go back and forth to the hospital in Salt Lake City every day. In addition, relatives and friends offered to help JoDee with her children by providing food, babysitting, rides to soccer games, and many other things needed to maintain family life.

Ryan made amazing progress every day. He remained in the intensive care unit for five days and then spent a couple days in a regular hospital room, where they helped him start eating and standing. After that, he was moved to the physical therapy wing, where he began receiving services to help him walk again with the aid of crutches.

After only three weeks in the hospital, Ryan was released to go home. With only a few setbacks, he made an amazing recovery and continues to recover to this day.

I marvel at how so many lives, including mine, have been touched by the miracles that occurred during that time. There were many people whose thoughts, actions, and prayers made it possible for JoDee, Ryan, and their family to heal from this traumatic experience. I truly believe there are angels who walk among us and help bring about the Lord's miracles. It is impossible to express the amount of gratitude we felt for the hand of the Lord in saving Ryan's life. I know the Lord watches over each of us and blesses us in our time of need.

My testimony was strengthened during that time, and again, a few months later, as I attended JoDee and Ryan's ward to be part of the celebration of their daughter's baptism and their son's priesthood ordination. I watched as Ryan walked slowly but independently to the podium to bear his testimony, and I was filled with a great joy that Heavenly Father had blessed our family with the gift of life. Ryan had survived an accident that should have taken his life, and he was there that day to be part of his children's lives and perform sacred ordinances for them.

Kelly Clark is a single mother of five children. She attended Utah State University and received her M.S. and Ed.S. degrees in school psychology. She now works for a large school district in Utah and loves to work with children. She is actively involved in her ward and happily serves in Primary. Family, immediate and extended, is the single-most important and motivating force in her life.

I will be on your right hand and on your left, and my
Spirit shall be in your hearts, and mine angels
round about you, to bear you up.

—D&C 84:88

Held Back

By Brian G. Shelley

My companion and I were serving in the Connecticut Hartford Mission. It was sometime during the summer of 1988 that we found ourselves working in Fair Haven, an area of great diversity. The neighborhoods in our assigned area were varied and included most ethnic groups, including blacks, Hispanics, Italians, Russians, Jews, and other minorities.

Most blocks consisted of very old row houses that rose four or five stories above the street, some with weathered front porches. These rundown buildings lined the streets, and teenagers often hung out on corners and doorsteps. Gangs were prevalent. Most ethnic groups kept close to their own turf and tended not to mix with each other. As a result, residents were extremely wary of two white men wearing suits who walked into their areas, and it wasn't uncommon for us to be mistaken for officers of some kind.

My companion and I were meeting with member families and giving them short presentations. One faithful family lived on the ground floor in one of the Hispanic housing units. They had invited us over for dinner and one of our missionary presentations. Although not wealthy by worldly standards, they were rich in spirit and often welcomed us into their home. We generally arrived during daylight hours and did not linger after dark.

That evening we hopped on the usual Bella Vista bus that took us along a route that looped through the rough neighborhood where the family lived and then back again to a stop near our apartment, also in a rather run-down building. We neared the stop closest to our dinner appointment, and I was preparing to stand up when suddenly, inexplicably, I felt a pressure against my chest that literally held me immobile. The pressure was so powerful that I could not turn my head or lift my arm. It felt as if a force had gripped my heart, and I wondered if I was going to die. I could not move or speak.

We passed the bus stop, and I was so overcome with the pressure holding me back that I tried to glance at my companion to explain why we had missed our stop, but I could barely move my head, let alone talk. We traveled on. Finally, it was too late to hop off and rush back in time to make our dinner visit.

As the bus continued on its way, the force gradually receded, and the pressure on my chest let up. Had I had some kind of attack? Was I ill? I could not explain it. In time, we arrived back at our original stop close to our apartment, and my companion and I got up and left the bus.

We looked at each other with the same question on our minds: what just happened? It turned out both of us had experienced the *very same sensation*. Neither one of us had been able to move from our seat.

When we got back to our apartment, I called the family to explain.

"We've been trying to reach you!" exclaimed the wife. "There is a terrible shoot-out going on outside on the street tonight between gang members and police! Some of them are on our front porch, and we are huddled down on the floor even now. We've been trying to call you to warn you not to come!"

We realized the Lord had been watching over His servants. That night we gave thanks for the protective power that had surrounded us and prevented us from walking into a gun battle where we surely would have been mistaken for law enforcement officers. I know the Lord watches over His missionaries, and that night we knew He had extended His great love and care to two missionaries just trying their best to carry light into darkened lives.

Brian Shelley lives in Clinton, Iowa, with his wife and four children. He enjoys travel and family activities.

Verily, verily, I say unto you, I will impart unto you of my Spirit, which shall enlighten your mind, which shall fill your soul with joy.

—D&C 11:13

Building the Kingdom in My Heart

By Shirley Manning

When I was sixteen years old, the members of our ward had the opportunity to help with the construction of our own meetinghouse. Many Mutual nights were devoted to one activity—building our new chapel. While adult ward members and professional builders completed the parts that took skill and know-how, all the youth were given jobs suited to their strength and abilities. The boys were organized to carry and stack materials, sand, paint, stain, and get rid of debris. We girls did much of the same work, except for hauling heavy materials.

The walls of the new church were cinderblock. We spent many hours rolling pale yellow paint on those walls. The leaders didn't seem to care that we dripped a lot of pastel paint on the concrete floors. They must have had a lot of faith in the Lord's plan for our chapel. (Just think of a bunch of high school kids, each with a roller and a pan of gooey paint!)

We sanded and stained the huge beams that would arch above our heads in the chapel. We learned that the coarse sandpaper was a kind of emery board for wooden beams—and for the skin on our fingers if we weren't careful. We breathed in the fine dust we sanded out of the beams, coughed a little, and laughed a lot because we loved working together. Our hands took on the dark walnut tone of the stain, but it eventually wore off with the help of some pungent turpentine.

Over weeks and months, our church building took shape. One of our last projects was to sand and stain the benches in the chapel. Things were becoming real for us now as we imagined sitting on those benches in sacrament meeting in only a few short weeks. Workers soon laid the carpet, covering our messy paint spills. And finally, all other finishing touches were completed, including cleaning the windows and vacuuming the floors.

We were excited to present our new building to the ward members, local Church priesthood leaders, and the Lord.

When the announcement came for the dedication, my friend Julie and I decided we couldn't miss it. We all assembled in the chapel at the appointed hour. Julie and I chose a bench we had sanded and painted ourselves and quietly sat down. My feelings of excitement turned to more reverent feelings as the organ music filled the chapel and the commotion of people arriving and being seated calmed. It was both awe-inspiring and humbling to sit in a finished meetinghouse I had helped build.

I don't remember who spoke at that first meeting in our chapel. I don't remember what songs we sang or even who gave the dedicatory prayer. What I do remember and have always cherished is the feeling I had during that prayer.

For the dedicatory prayer, we were all invited to kneel at our bench. My life was blessed during that prayer in a way that would have been unimaginable to me just minutes before. As I listened to the prayer, I became aware of the sweetest feeling I had ever had up to that point in my life. I felt tears on my cheeks as I realized we were in the Lord's house. It wasn't just those cinderblock walls dowsed with yellow paint or oak beams smoothed and stained or even the new carpet on which we knelt.

It was the Lord's house. To me, it was as if He had come personally to say to each one of us, "Well done." I was so enveloped by this feeling of joy and awe that I felt as if He were truly there. I did not open my eyes, but I thought that if I had opened them, I could have seen the Savior right there and then.

From that moment to this, I have recognized my experience as a wonderful gift. So strong was the Spirit that testified of the reality of Jesus Christ and His love for me and all others that I have never doubted His existence, His place at the head of His Church, or His obedience to God the Father. To think that at the young age of sixteen I had been given the blessing of a sure testimony of the divinity of Jesus Christ is humbling and marvelous, for I have relied on that witness many times in my life. And I remind myself from time to time as I sit comfortably on a bench in a chapel someone else has built that I am in a holy edifice dedicated to God.

Shirley Manning resides in Kaysville, Utah, with her husband, Marty. They have one son, five daughters, five sons-in-law, and fourteen grandchildren. Her greatest joy is time spent with them.

I will not leave you comfortless.

—John 14:18

Two Comforters

By Bonnie Smith

In 2002, my husband set up an appointment for me at the Mayo Clinic in Rochester, Minnesota. He even asked my dear friend Kellie, who lived in another state, to go with me. My neck was twisting, pulling my head uncomfortably and uncontrollably up and to the left. It was causing me a lot of pain and discomfort, and we wanted a diagnosis and the best help we could get.

The clinic determined I had a dystonia (muscle abnormality) called spastic torticollis. In order to find out which muscles were in constant contraction and having spasms, I had to be hooked up to a machine by having twenty-two needles placed in my neck muscles. I was told it would be only slightly painful. On the day of the treatment, I agreed to meet Kellie later on for dinner. Then I went to the clinic.

As it turned out, the treatment wasn't just "slightly painful." It was excruciating! As they placed each needle, one at a time, in my neck, I felt a burning pain. They looked at my agony-filled face. "It shouldn't hurt so much," they told me. But I have always been extremely sensitive to pain, and I felt the sting of each needle acutely. With tears in my eyes, I endured the best I could until it was finally over. The whole process left me spent.

If that weren't enough, after the needles were finally removed, the doctors gave me seven shots of Botox in the contracting muscles. Each injection was so very painful! When they finished, they all walked out with the usual chatter amongst themselves and left me alone in the room. For them, the job was done. But I was physically a wreck and emotionally wiped out, and I was all alone, trembling in the aftermath of the ordeal. I felt violated. My neck felt violated. There was no one to turn to or to comfort me.

Tears filled my eyes once again. After months of suffering, straining to hold my head straight, fighting against this awful force that wanted to painfully twist my head over to my shoulder, I had to endure this—this pain-filled procedure done with the knowledge that botox shots had little lasting effect because the medical field offered no cure for my problem! I felt completely undone, both emotionally and physically. How I wished Kellie had come with me.

As I wallowed in pain and disappointment, a most beautiful thing happened. I felt a presence in the room that filled my whole body from head to toe. I experienced the most wonderful feeling of the Savior's love and peace.

The Lord had heard my prayers and had magnificently encompassed me with His love. I was finally able to get up and walk into the waiting room, where, to my astonishment, I found my friend Kellie waiting for me. Immediately, she came to me and wrapped me in her arms.

I started to cry. I felt that I had been passed from one angel to another. That day I had been comforted from both sides of the veil.

It took many years of prayers, a promise of healing given in a priesthood blessing, and some surprising twists and turns I felt guided to take before my neck muscles stopped contracting. But today I can walk with my head straight. I know the journey started that day at the Mayo Clinic, and it has been guided at every step by the Lord, who has sent me many earthly angels as well as heavenly comforts throughout this journey. I know there are angels both seen and unseen who bless and help us through this life.

Bonnie Smith lives in Kennewick, Washington, with her husband, Sam. They have five children, two in high school and three attending Brigham Young University. Bonnie enjoys her family, playing games, the ocean, mountains, gardening, swimming, basketball, volleyball, and exploring natural ways to be healthy.

Seek diligently to turn the hearts of the children to their fathers, and the hearts of the fathers to the children.

—D&C 98:16

Not Alone

By Robynn Sisam

After my children grew up and married, I found myself living alone. However, I had the wonderful privilege of serving as a temple worker in the Jordan River Temple. I would stand quietly, greeting people and showing them where to go.

Many times family groups would come in with large smiles and hugs for everyone. I especially felt a pang of jealousy whenever I saw mothers and daughters going through together. I envied their close-knit families. You see, my father had passed away the year before, and my mother was not active. Although my children had all married in the temple, they were busy with young families and could not attend with me very often.

For many reasons, I just wanted my mother by my side in that sacred place. I wanted the warmth of love and sisterhood to flow between us. I wanted the sense of family and belonging I saw in others.

One day I was preparing to do an endowment session. I headed for the chapel on the second floor, and as I was riding up the escalator, I heard my father's voice in my mind say, *Robynn, I know your mother can't be here, but I can be here and go to the session with you.*

That day, I too felt the warmth and love of family with me in the temple. I was very grateful for this comfort, and I felt the Lord was truly mindful of me in a way I had never really expected. He knew of my deep, unspoken longing and allowed my father to be with me on that very special day.

Robynn Sisam, a resident of Sandy, Utah, is mother of five and grandmother of eleven. She enjoys playing with her grandchildren and taking care of her dog and three cats.

Look unto God with firmness of mind, and pray unto him with exceeding faith, and he will console you in your afflictions.

—Jacob 3:1

Consolation

By Frances Pershing

I had grown up with the idea that once people marry, they deal with whatever comes. My husband and I met while he was in the service, and we married quickly. He left for Germany a few days after our wedding. Later, after he got out of the service, we finally settled down and had two children. At first I thought things would work out, but as the years went by, his temper began to take a toll on the family. Then he began accusing me of many weird things, none of which were happening. He even began putting tape on the door to see if I was leaving the house or if someone entered while he was gone.

I had grown up believing we were told to stay married for the sake of the children and that divorce hurts children. I bore it the best I could. The final straw came one day when I came home from work early, not feeling well. As I walked back to our bedroom, I heard him on the phone saying, "I haven't asked for a divorce yet because she'll want an arm and a leg." I was shocked to find out that he had been having an affair behind my back. I quietly went back to the kitchen, and when he came out, I told him he could have his divorce. I let him know I did not want "an arm and a leg," not even a finger or a toe. I wanted nothing from him but my own things. We both got separate lawyers. His lawyer told mine that my husband was a nutcase. When my husband didn't show up at court, the divorce was granted.

I was working full time, and although it was difficult and even frightening in many ways to have sole financial responsibility, I was relieved to have the marriage end. However, I had not understood what the years of abuse had done to our two children.

Soon after the divorce, my daughter came to me and told me that she was glad for the divorce because she had been molested from the time she was very young, possibly as young as three years old. Her dad told her she couldn't tell me because then I would hate her. I was heartsick. Physical abuse leaves physical scars. Emotional scars are hidden deep in the heart. Sexual abuse has elements of both—the damage goes so very deep. How I mourned that I had not figured it out and protected my daughter.

My son, Patrick, a talented artist, was a deeply sensitive, spiritual boy. His father had come home from work before I did and had evidently said a lot of cruel and emotionally abusive things to our son. When I was home, I stopped that kind of talk. But I could not protect my son all the time. By the time of the divorce, our son had become addicted to drugs and alcohol. I was beside myself with worry and didn't understand all that had been going on.

Once I was on my own with our children, Patrick tried to get his life back in order. He hated his addiction and struggled to be rid of it. To fight it, he attended Alcoholics Anonymous meetings and started attending church again. He got a job to earn money to go on a mission. He talked to the bishop and was eventually ordained an elder. It looked like he was going to be okay.

I took him to see the stake patriarch, and he was given a strong blessing that his mission would be very successful and the people he would convert would "rise up and call him blessed." The patriarch asked to be invited to his farewell. However, when Patrick went to the stake president to talk about serving a mission, the president, with inspired but unwelcome advice, told him he should wait at least a year or until his addiction was fully and finally over. While I was disappointed for Patrick, I knew it was the right thing to do.

Patrick decided to join the army. He did well, earning rewards and going to church at his army post. Then he was sent to Germany, where drugs were more easily available. After some problems, he was given a general discharge and came home to live with me.

In December 1992, I convinced him to go with me to Utah to visit my mom and sisters for Christmas. He hadn't seen them for many years, and he was in great spirits. He loved seeing his grandma again, and he cried over his granddad's grave. He had fun at the family Christmas dinner with cousins he had never met. We came home, and he wanted to go shopping for church clothes. He decided it was time to get his life together for good. In January 1993, he made an appointment with the bishop to start the repentance process.

On the night before he was to see the bishop, his life tragically ended. I'll never know exactly what happened that night. It appears he overdosed on a medication he was taking, because there were no street drugs in the room, and the autopsy found no other drugs in his body. The police report listed it as suicide. Of course, I was devastated, but I took comfort in the knowledge that he was not hurting anymore. Still, I worried about him. My understanding of suicide was that he had forfeited his eternal inheritance. Yet I couldn't believe that someone who was that spiritually minded when he was not on drugs or alcohol would be denied some sort of forgiveness by a loving and understanding Heavenly Father.

A few months later, I was preparing a lesson and got out a stack of old *Liahona* magazines. Choosing one at random, I opened it to an article on suicide. ("Suicide: Some Things We Know and Some We Do Not," by Elder M. Russell Ballard, March 1988.) Elder Ballard said that Heavenly Father is aware of the feelings of those who take their own life, and He takes all things into consideration. This gave me hope that Patrick would not spend eternity in darkness. A year after his death, I had his temple work done.

Although this helped me through the next several years, one day I was feeling particularly sad, and the thought of Patrick weighed on my mind. I knelt in prayer for consolation and asked for some way to know what he was doing. Was he okay? Was he in darkness? As I prayed, the most extraordinary experience unfolded before me. What seemed like a bolt of blue-white lightning entered the top of my head and spread throughout my whole body, bringing a feeling of warmth and peace along with a complete knowledge that Patrick was doing missionary work! With tears in my eyes, I thanked Heavenly Father for this understanding. I knew it was a confirmation of Patrick's patriarchal blessing—that through his missionary work, those departed souls he was teaching were calling him blessed.

I don't really know all the elements that affect eternal justice and judgment, but I do know Father in Heaven loves each of us and is acutely aware of the pressures and problems that govern our decisions. His understanding is so profound that I know we can rely on Him completely, no matter what, and that His love reaches out to bring hope and consolation to all of us. I will never forget the feeling of peace and knowledge that flooded me that day, and I have never again felt that Patrick's suicide ended his chances for peace.

Frances Hatch Pershing was born in Idaho, but she grew up in Green River and Rock Springs, Wyoming. After a semester at Brigham Young University, Frances's parents moved to Utah. Mother of two children, Frances now lives in Greensboro, North Carolina, where she enjoys reading, writing (mostly poetry), and painting. She loves to spend time with her four grandchildren and three great-grandchildren.

These things I have spoken unto you, that in me ye might have peace. In the world ye shall have tribulation: but be of good cheer; I have overcome the world.

—John 16:33

My First Day in the Philippines

By Sabine Berlin

The day I arrived in the Philippines as a missionary was one of the longest of my life. A twenty-two hour plane ride left me full of excitement and exhaustion. For the next seventeen months, I would be teaching the gospel of Jesus Christ and building friendships that would last for eternity. I was prepared for trials on my mission; I just didn't expect such a rush of them on my first day.

First, my camera broke, exposing all my pictures from my last day at the MTC. That was frustrating, but I could live with it. Then the intense pollution in Manila infected my eyes to the point that I could barely open them, and when I did, I couldn't see through the pus. With my eyes streaming, I had to make my way through a foreign airport practically blind. Once I arrived at the mission home, I didn't get to spend the night with the rest of the sisters who had arrived with me because someone who could give me a ride was heading out to my assigned area right away. In terrible exhaustion and with bleary eyes, I was rushed to my area when all I wanted was to stop and rest for a day.

On top of everything else, I found I had yet one more problem. I'd spent the last two months learning the closest language the MTC offered to the one spoken on this island. I soon realized it wasn't all that close. So by the time I arrived at my new apartment and met my companion, I was running on autopilot.

I headed straight over and collapsed on my bed. My head had not even found comfort on the lumpy pillow when it was time to leave for our night's appointments. At that moment, I was anything but delighted about the prospect of leaving the room for the next several hours. I needed sleep. I needed to give my eyes a chance to recuperate, and I needed time to unpack and settle in. I felt I needed time to take care of myself.

Amidst the haze of thoughts that beckoned me to take the night off, another thought settled firmly upon me. I felt as though a beam of light had broken through my weary and worn-out mind. I suddenly understood in a way that I had not thought possible that the only thing I actually needed was to go out and share the gospel. My time on this mission would not be infinite. I needed to spend every precious moment doing the Lord's work. This thought revived me. I opened my eyes. My head felt clearer, and with newfound energy, I hauled myself up, slid back into my sandals, and followed my companion into the humid night air.

In a way, that small decision set me on a course I pursued throughout my mission. I found that my physical stamina could go on a few more hours without rest and that the drops my mission president had prescribed were already soothing my eyes. I began to realize the importance of not giving up.

However, my challenges weren't over.

With my physical strength renewed, my mental ability now seemed to come under attack. Just the thought of attempting to teach the gospel in a language I knew nothing about terrified me. Then other thoughts began to plague me. How could I teach the gospel at all? What made me think people would even care what I said? Why had I thought I could be a missionary? The farther we walked from our apartment, the more these mental lashings began to wear me down.

We arrived at an area known as a squatter village. Makeshift houses put together with scraps of metal, plywood, and even cardboard were jammed as closely as possible over a thick layer of dirt and grime that produced a nauseating smell. It was dark outside, and most of the village had no electricity. The hut we came to was nothing more than a few pieces of wood covered with a plastic liner for the roof. The floor was dirt. A small cloth separated the sleeping area from the front room, which contained only a tiny table with two poorly constructed benches and a few dishes in the corner.

We sat down on one of the rickety benches and began to share a passage from the Book of Mormon. A small gas lamp made from a jam jar and a piece of rope lighted the words. Across the room, a cat-sized rat ran between the small gap that separated the wall and the plastic sheet. I tried to concentrate on the words as a cockroach scurried over my open-toed sandal. I prayed for understanding as small flying ants kept getting stuck in my hair. The people a few houses down had managed to get electricity to their hut for their radio. As Kenny Rogers and Dolly Parton began to sing "Islands in the Stream" at a deafening volume, I was convinced I had made a big mistake. I felt awful, I didn't understand a single word, and I could barely concentrate from all the commotion surrounding me. I wasn't sure how I was going to accomplish all I wanted to when I couldn't even make it through one evening.

And then my companion bore her testimony.

Suddenly, the room was filled with the Spirit of the Lord. That sweet Spirit wrapped me in its embrace, and my mind cleared. In words I could not understand, the message of gospel hope my companion shared became evident in our investigators' eyes, and it filled my heart too. All these things that had seemed to pile up on me were fleeting. My camera would likely make it through the rest of my mission with the help of duct tape, my eyes were already starting to recover, my ability to learn the language would surely improve with time and practice, and one day I knew I could be more effective in sharing the gospel. The darkness that had walked by my side for hours lifted. I knew then that I could find joy even in trying circumstances and the most humble conditions.

I had other trials on my mission and have continued to encounter them throughout my life as well. But on that night, I learned that once I decide to go forward in faith, despite multiple challenges, no matter where I am in my life or in the world, the Lord will be there for me. All I need to do is let Him in.

Sabine Berlin served in the Philippines Bacolod Mission. After several years as a stay-at-home mom, she has recently gone back to school at Utah Valley University, where she is studying history. She enjoys writing, traveling, and spending time with her family. She lives in Provo, Utah, with her husband and three children.

Put Your Trust in That Spirit Which Leadeth to Do Good.

—D&C 11:12

Yet learned he obedience by the things which he suffered.

—Hebrews 5:8

Learning the Hard Way

By Maria Serafini de Ozuna

Our home in Paraguay had a number of rooms built off a central patio. We rented out some of the rooms, so we often had people coming and going. The communal bath was also located in a room off the central patio.

One day my daughter, recently turned fifteen, passed me as she headed across the patio to take a shower. She suddenly realized she was still wearing a precious and expensive gold watch, one her aunt had saved up for a year to buy for her *quinceañera*, or fifteenth birthday celebration, which is traditionally a young woman's most important day.

On the patio was a huge mango tree. I was outside using a long pole to poke at a large mango to try to get it to fall. As my daughter passed me, she took off the watch and set it on the windowsill of the rental unit next to the mango tree then went in to shower.

As I kept nudging the fruit, a thought came clearly to my mind: *Take care of the watch!*

I continued to push at the fruit, thinking, *Okay, as soon as I get the mango to drop.*

Again the impression came: *Take care of the watch!*

I stayed focused on the mango, which was being very stubborn. Again, a third time, the impression came. About then the mango finally dropped. Relieved, I picked it up and carried it to the kitchen.

A few minutes later I heard my daughter call, "Mother, hand me my watch!"

I suddenly recalled the impressions I'd received and ran outside. The watch was gone!

We searched carefully inside and out. We questioned our renters. But we could not find the watch, the precious watch.

How could I have not listened? I was devastated that I had ignored the promptings.

Years have passed, and the pain of that loss stays with me even today. But I learned a difficult and important lesson.

Sometime later, my mother came to live with us. She had dementia and was very hard to care for. During the first few months she was in our home, she simply wandered away on a number of occasions. So we kept a close eye on her.

One place we often went to visit was my sister Juanita's home, just two blocks away. On this particular day, I noticed my mother had left the house, so I quickly stepped outside. I saw her walking a block away, heading for Juanita's place. Since I had dinner cooking and my husband coming home soon, I was under some pressure to have the meal ready for him.

As I returned to the kitchen to finish cooking dinner, I had the strongest impression come over me: *Go find your mother!*

This time, I didn't hesitate. I turned and ran from the house, heading to the corner where I had last seen her. She was nowhere in sight! Instead of crossing the street and continuing on to Juanita's place, Mother must have turned the corner. As my eyes searched, I saw three different streets she could have taken, and from where I stood, I didn't see her on any of them. What was I to do?

Then a thought came clearly to me: *Take the road that leads to the meetinghouse.* Our chapel was located a good half-hour's walk from the house. Had Mother tried to go there? It wasn't very close, so I worried even more. I took off running and followed the road for nearly twenty minutes before I finally caught up with my mother. How she had gone so far in so short a time amazed me. Although she did not want to come with me, I finally managed to bring her back to the house.

If I had not listened, I don't know what might have happened to my mother. In her confusion, she might have wandered the streets for hours or even days. I am so grateful to have received a prompting that allowed me to bring my mother safely home again.

And although the loss of the watch hurt very much, the lesson I learned was not forgotten. Because of that experience, I knew what it felt like to receive promptings from the Holy Ghost, and I knew the importance of responding to them immediately. That knowledge helped me save my mother from danger.

María Ozuna and her husband, Feliciano, are parents of five children and have five grandchildren. They live in Draper, Utah, where they enjoy their family and work faithfully in the Church.

O that ye would listen unto the word of his commands.

—Jacob 2:16

The Blessings of Listening

By Travis Behunin

While I served as a missionary in the California Santa Rosa mission, I had two experiences that taught me the value of listening.

The first experience took place near Cordelia, California. Our assigned district covered three cities: Green Valley, Cordelia, and old Suisun. We were living in a guesthouse behind the home of a member family, the Grazands, who lived along a country road outside Cordelia. Brother and Sister Grazand had met a few years earlier. Upon hearing the gospel, Marco had become converted, and after his baptism, the couple had married.

From that time on, Marco always loved having missionaries around, so he invited them to live in a small guest house behind the main house. Because the family lived on a country road between the three cities we covered, we found living at the Grazands' enjoyable as well as convenient. Each day as we traveled between cities, we were blessed with some of the most splendid scenery around.

The Grazands' home sat near the steep bank of a gully that had a river running through it. Many pine trees and shrubs grew along the gully. As winter approached, the river swelled, almost filling the gully to overflowing. It was not uncommon for the country road we traveled on to have a foot or two of water covering it in spots. One night it rained so hard that the river rose higher than usual, washing away part of the bank with it. A huge pine tree came crashing down, smashing through a fence on the other side of the bank.

A few days later, Elder Otto and I were in our apartment having lunch when we heard a crying sound, like a bird or animal. We thought nothing of it and finished our lunch. But as we left our apartment, we heard the sound again. I stopped my companion, and we listened. He said it was most likely a bird. We started to walk away, but a feeling came over me, and I stopped. Now that we were outside, the sound did not seem like an animal anymore. At that moment, I had a strong impression that I needed to find out what was making the sound.

I motioned to my companion, Elder Otto, to come with me. We reached the river bank, and there we found a little girl, maybe three or four years old, hanging onto a mat of grass on the other side of the bank, dangerously close to the swirling water. She had managed to climb through the fence where the tree had broken through and wandered too close to the edge of the riverbank. She had slipped and fallen at least fifteen feet, nearly plunging into the water. If she lost her hold, the river current was so strong that it likely would have carried her away.

We looked at each other, unsure of how to reach her. We were wearing our missionary suits and dress shoes. A thousand thoughts came to mind, including whether there was time to cross to the other side by running to the bridge. I pushed that thought aside because the bridge was too far away. Could we cross on the fallen tree? I glanced at my shoes, wondering if they would slip on the wet wood. Then Elder Otto remembered seeing Brother Grazand out in his workshop and raced off to get him. In moments, Elder Otto was back with Marco, who was dressed in work boots and sturdy clothing.

Taking no thought for his own safety, Marco rushed across the slippery, wet tree and plunged down the muddy river bank, scooping up the child. He then returned the girl to her own backyard.

I think of the chain of events that led to saving her life that day. If Brother Grazand had not joined the Church, we would not have been there that day to hear the cries of the little girl. And then, when we did hear her cries, it would have been so easy to shrug off the sounds as something of no real importance. But instead, I listened, and we acted immediately.

I used to think a hero was only a fireman or a policeman. However, I came to learn that average people like you and me—and the Brother Grazands of this world—can be heroes, if we listen and obey.

Later, when I had been on my mission for little more than a year, I had another experience with listening. Only this was a little different. Our mission president decided that one day a month we would leave our cars and bikes at home and walk. This, he assured us, would help us gain a better perspective on how life was for the early Saints. Some of the trials we faced, he explained, paled in comparison to theirs. It would be good for us.

This was not greeted with a lot of enthusiasm. My companion, for one, loved riding his bike and was heard—thankfully not too loudly—grumbling about this. How would the mission president ever know if we used our bikes or not? However, his complaining didn't work, and when the day came, we set out on foot. We went tracting and kept a few appointments, just as we normally did, although at a slower pace.

By afternoon, we had reached the downtown area of Vallejo and began talking to people we passed on our way to an appointment. A man stopped us who looked gruff and not very happy to see us. He said he knew who we were, that we were missionaries of The Church of Jesus Christ of Latter-day Saints, and that he had talked to some elders before. Then he became menacing and demanded that we pay him for his time spent listening to the other elders! In fact, he demanded our bikes as payment.

Shocked, we were honest with him and told him we didn't have them with us. He thought maybe we had chained them up somewhere close by and demanded that we take him to where we had left them. When we explained that the bikes were at home, I thought he might get violent. It was a tense situation, and I wondered if maybe he would steal our wallets or beat us up, but he didn't. As I stood there confronting this bully, I felt a peace enter my heart, and my companion later told me he did as well. We knew he would not harm us. The man suddenly changed his mind and backed off, letting us go.

If we had not listened to and obeyed our mission president's inspired counsel to walk that day, I have no doubt we would have lost our bikes—and maybe more. Sometimes the Lord asks us to do things, and we don't understand why. We might even feel as though we are just being punished for some reason. But that is only because we can't see the big picture.

These two events taught me the importance of simply listening—listening to a prompting to check a riverbank and listening to counsel from our priesthood leaders. Both kinds of listening brought safety in dangerous circumstances. Learning to trust the Lord is vital today. It often means we must listen and obey, even when we do not know why.

Travis Behunin has recently returned to college in hope of obtaining an education degree in mathematics. He enjoys the outdoors, reading, writing, going to movies, and spending time with his nieces and nephew.

Pray in your families unto the Father, always in my name, that your wives and your children may be blessed.

—3 Nephi 18:21

Would Jeffrey Survive?

By Cheri Chesley

My husband and I were ecstatic when my second pregnancy resulted in twins and I delivered two adorable baby boys—Jeffrey and Daniel. That joy soon turned to concern when we noticed a problem with Jeffrey.

When he was only ten days old, Jeffrey made his first trip to the emergency room. I had been at home nursing both babies when Jeffrey spewed dark green vomit all over the three of us. The doctor at the hospital assured me my son was fine. He had been born three and a half weeks premature, and I should expect problems, he said. These things usually sort themselves out as babies mature.

At age twenty-three, I was well conditioned to trust that doctors knew what they were talking about. The emergency room doctor didn't lack sincerity and certainly behaved as though he spoke the truth, but I could not relax. A gnawing, persistent doubt formed within me and whispered that something was very wrong with my son, and it should not be ignored. So I went to see my pediatrician. I soon learned, however, that convincing her would not be easy. At every visit, I talked to the doctor about Jeffrey's vomiting. I explained that Daniel only spit up; Jeffrey lost almost everything. Why wouldn't she listen? The doctor continued to assure me both babies' digestive systems were immature, and they would both grow out of it.

While Jeffrey continued to vomit after nearly every meal, I gradually adapted to this new reality. I would feed him several hours before leaving the house so he could have his "episode," and I would clean him before we left. I stopped nursing the boys and put them on formula, then soy formula, but nothing changed Jeffrey's habits. Though the boys grew, Jeffrey remained steadily smaller than Daniel. Also, while Daniel thrived, Jeffrey just survived.

Because Jeffrey still registered low-normal on the baby growth charts and the doctor had never seen him vomit, she remained convinced he would outgrow this problem. I, however, developed a habit of constant prayer for Jeffrey and kept a prayer in my mind every waking hour. I knew something was wrong with him, but without clear evidence the doctors would do nothing.

Months passed, and my concern only deepened. What could I do if the doctors refused to believe there was a problem? I prayed that if Jeffrey was indeed in trouble, as my heart told me, his doctors would understand that. Then, at nine months, Jeffrey spent some time in the hospital for dehydration. We had gone on a road trip, and the combination of the drive and the vomiting had put him in distress. Soon after, at his nine-month checkup, the doctor noted for the first time that my son had lost some ground on the growth chart. She told me any digestive problems should have resolved themselves by now, and my son would need testing to determine the cause of his decline.

At last!

We took him to be tested, and the test showed a blockage just under his stomach. We would need a second test to determine exactly how to approach the blockage and what could be done. This second test could only be done at the children's hospital an hour and a half away, and the only appointment I could arrange was four weeks away. Despite my reservations that it was too long a wait, I felt I had no choice but to take it.

Because Jeffrey was declining, we counted off the days and weeks, hoping he would make it until he could be tested. Then, the Monday before Jeffrey's scheduled appointment, I had to take him to the emergency room again. By six that evening, he hadn't wet his diaper in more than twelve hours.

Friends met me at the hospital and took care of my two other boys while Jeffrey and I saw the doctor. The medical personnel had trouble getting an IV in him and, eventually, after nearly two hours of poking him with needles, finally inserted an IV into his shin. The emergency room doctor contacted Jeffrey's doctor, and together they decided he should go to the children's hospital that night. I rode on the ambulance stretcher with him because he was too small to ride safely on it alone.

They wheeled us into the children's hospital emergency room at about 1:30 a.m. It took about three hours for them to admit him, evaluate him, and give him a bed on the fourth-floor surgery wing. By five in the morning, Jeffrey had been settled in bed with a new IV in his arm, held in place with arm splints to prevent him from pulling it out. He managed to pull it out anyway.

They tested him Tuesday, located the obstruction, and scheduled surgery for Thursday. Wednesday, Jeffrey again managed to pull out his IV. No one in the hospital could get another one in him, including the nurse who regularly inserted IVs into patients while flying in the rescue helicopter. The doctors told me they would have to put one in his shoulder for the surgery, so they would wait until then.

For a little while, my baby wasn't hooked up with wires and tubes, and I was able to hold him. My husband, Bryan, held him. We sang to him. We walked with him. We loved him. Then we took him to the pre-op room.

I can't describe exactly how I felt when the time came to hand Jeffrey over to the surgeons. I had fought for ten months to see him to this point and keep him alive. Now I had to turn his life over to strangers and trust that they would save him. I had to believe they could.

The closer we got to surgery, the more my persistent feelings of worry and dread eased. Even though it was hard, I knew we had chosen the right option. Jeffrey would eventually die without the surgery. And even though the surgery had risks, it would be my son's best option for survival. The doctors still weren't sure what they would find when they opened him. They would have to make a large incision so they could make a correct diagnosis and then determine the best course once they understood the problem.

Bryan and I were sent to a waiting room, where other groups of parents sat huddled in much the same state we were, reading magazines and trying to keep busy while waiting. I stared for a long time at a magazine page without seeing it. Though I felt in my heart my son would make it, I also felt doubt creeping into my thoughts. Doubt is a very difficult feeling to suppress. Every so often, the phone would ring, and a few minutes later the receptionist would call out someone's name. Finally, it was our turn. The surgeon would be out in a few moments to tell us what had happened.

We soon found out that when Jeffrey and Daniel had formed in the womb, cells that were supposed to be part of something else in his anatomy had formed within Jeffrey's intestinal cells. This resulted in a damaged section of duodenal (small) intestine, where the walls were so thickened that only a pin-sized opening allowed food to pass through. The surgeon explained that to correct the problem, they had bypassed the problematic section entirely by slicing into and joining the areas above and below it.

Unfortunately, in order to get to the area, they had had to move some of his other organs, which resulted in his appendix becoming detached and free floating. They made the decision to remove the appendix entirely as a preventative step in case Jeffrey ever got appendicitis. If they had left his free-floating appendix inside his body, it might have ruptured before any doctor could properly diagnose him with appendicitis.

Exploratory surgery does not leave a dainty little scar. When I saw Jeffrey, he had a three-inch incision across his abdomen. But to me, it was one of the most beautiful things I have ever seen. It's almost as glorious as the memory I have of that same little boy two years later hiking his shirt up to his ears to point at his scar that saved his "wife."

Jeffrey had a follow-up appointment with his surgeon a month later. He received a clean bill of health, and the surgeon assured me he should suffer no problems as he got older. He would be able to live a normal life. Weeks later, around the twins' first birthday, Jeffrey's eating habits transformed essentially into that of any normal boy. Up to that time, he would eat for me but would refuse liquids in every form. This day, the difference was noticeable. My mother came for the twins' birthday and brought a water bottle the airline had given her. Jeffrey loved it and drank almost exclusively from that bottle for weeks.

That summer Daniel developed a sort of birthmark, or skin spot, on his left shoulder that matched the scar Jeffrey had in the same spot from his IV needle. They are less visible now, but I will never forget it. Every time I find myself getting frustrated with Jeffrey's behavior, I remember he almost wasn't here. I can't help but get a bit reflective every year as the anniversary of his surgery draws near. It's almost like a second birthday for Jeffrey.

I know the Lord guided me to get help for my son. I have learned that the Spirit can give impressions so plain that they are like one person speaking to another. Yet at other times, help also comes with only a steady feeling that something needs to be done. I never could have made it through the trial without the spiritual support I felt from the Lord that not only guided me in helping my son but also sustained me through every step.

Cheri Chesley, mother of five, resides in Tooele, Utah, where she is a daycare provider, author, and Primary worker. If she had spare time, she'd enjoy reading, baking, and photography. View her website at www.cherichesley.com.

And whatsoever they shall speak when moved upon by the Holy Ghost . . . shall be the will of the Lord.

—D&C 68:4

I Responded Immediately

Name Withheld

As a bishop in California, I would get promptings from time to time that I needed to visit with a certain person, couple, or family. I generally did not know why, but the uncomfortable feeling would persist until I met with the people involved. Yet, oftentimes as I waited, I wondered, was this the Lord's prompting or my own idea? Scary.

One Sunday morning as we were having our early morning bishopric meetings, I had one of those feelings that would not go away. I finally stopped, looked at my counselors, and asked if either of them knew something I should know. Of course they did not. The meeting continued, and the feeling persisted. Part of my mind continued to work on the problem, and I knew at last where to start the process.

As we ended the meeting, I explained to my counselors that I felt I needed to meet with the Young Women president—but I did not know why. I asked my executive secretary to call her and make an appointment to meet with her before sacrament meeting.

As I waited for her to come in, I felt my anxiety build as I wondered what I was going to say. It is absolutely scary sometimes to be a bishop and feel you really don't know why you are asking to meet with people. Relying on the Spirit takes a lot of faith, and I hoped that day that I was doing the right thing.

She came in the door, and I called her by name and indicated that she could sit down. Then I admitted that I did not know exactly what the meeting was about but that I kept having a feeling I had to meet with her. I looked expectantly at her and waited.

This dear sister started crying. Of course, as a bishop, a number of ideas went through my mind. First, of course, I had been right to bring her in. But tears? I thought, *Oh no. Now what?*

This sister admitted that in her heart she had very much wanted to meet with me. Even her husband had said she should call me—that I was an understanding person. But she had hesitated.

Now I really started getting nervous. She was the role model for the young women of the ward.

But then she explained. Her father was dying. He lived in Southern California, several hundred miles away, and she felt she had to leave immediately to help for an indefinite length of time. But what would become of her young women? Should her counselors carry on without her? What should she do?

Immediately, I felt concern about this heavy burden of grief and worry that had been placed on her shoulders. And I knew right then what I needed to do as her bishop. I told her I would release her *that very day* so she could leave in the morning. We would find a new presidency immediately, and she need not worry about it.

She cried with relief.

I felt a deep gratitude to our Heavenly Father, who blessed me with the prompting that morning to call in a sister without any idea why and who then granted me the gift of discernment to know what to do without a minute's hesitation—not my usual style.

Some months later, after her father died and things settled down for her, I knew she was to be called to serve as our ward Relief Society president. She remained in that calling long after I was released.

What if I had not listened to the prompting? It would have been so easy to dismiss it, since my nature is to carefully question every little thought. But I learned—and am still learning—that when I receive a prompting, I should always act and simply trust that the Lord will allow events to unfold in their own appropriate way, if I am willing to respond.

But behold, I, Nephi, will show unto you that
the tender mercies of the Lord are over all those whom
he hath chosen, because of their faith, to make them
mighty even unto the power of deliverance.

—1 Nephi 1:20

Check on Her!

By Sam Smith

Twenty-five years ago, as a student at the University of Nevada, Las Vegas, I was serving as the elders quorum president in our ward, which was a typical family ward since the university campus didn't have student wards at that time. I was notified one Sunday late in May of a new ward member, a single sister, who would be moving into an apartment within the ward boundaries at the end of the week.

My typical routine for Friday afternoons after school was to hang out at the institute, play ping-pong, talk to friends, relax, and eat some ice cream. This particular Friday, I arrived at the institute as usual. Just as I sat down to relax, I received a strong impression to check on our new ward member. My only means of transportation was my bicycle, so I rode over to the apartment building. It was a hot afternoon, and I was sweating when I arrived.

I knocked on the door, but there was no response. I stood there a moment, waiting, but no one came. Just as I was about to leave, I thought I heard a faint cry for help coming from inside the apartment! I quickly tried the door handle, and to my surprise, the door opened. I looked inside and found an elderly woman struggling for breath and overheated, with no one home to help. I found out she was the mother of our newest ward member. The woman explained that her daughter had left a couple hours earlier to get the utilities (phone, water, and power) hooked up, and she had not yet returned.

There was no water for her to drink and no electricity to operate her ventilation machine, which she needed to use from time to time to help her breathe. The heat had worsened her condition to a critical point. Because I had only my bike for transportation, I was relieved when she told me she had a car outside. I was able to take this woman to my apartment, get her some cool water to drink, and plug in her machine for her. We left a short note for her daughter to let her know what had happened.

I believe a very sad accident was narrowly avoided because of the tender mercies of the Lord. I am grateful for the opportunity I had to help a woman in need. The Lord surely knows all our hearts and all our needs, and He is there to help us through life's many unplanned circumstances.

Sam Smith lives in Kennewick, Washington, with his wife, Bonnie. Sam works as an electrical engineer, programming programmable logic controllers for automation and control systems. They have five children, one in high school, two attending Brigham Young University, one on a mission in Florida, and one pursuing a master's degree in Ireland. Sam enjoys his family, Scouting, exercise, and ice cream.

Prove me now herewith, saith the Lord of hosts, if
I will not open you the windows of heaven,
and pour you out a blessing.

—Malachi 3:10

Tithing . . . or Rent?

By Judy C. Olsen

I turned ten years old the year life changed for me forever. There were only six of us living at home at the time, my parents and four children: Carol, Doug, Sara, and me. Two of my sisters had already married. We had just moved to a small town in the Midwest, leaving behind a large, beautiful home in Seattle, Washington, as well as extended family members, friends, and years of meaningful Church callings.

My sister Sara and I started at a new school in Waukegan, Illinois; Douglas started at a new high school; and my sister Carol, who had just turned eighteen, was planning on going to college. We didn't know anyone in that small town, of course. I felt my world had turned upside down. But as things go, that was only the beginning.

Not long after we moved into an old two-story house on a tree-shaded street, my dad was hospitalized. One night after I had gone to bed and fallen sound asleep, I was shaken awake by my sister Carol. "Our daddy has just died," she told me gently. "You need to come downstairs." He was only forty-six years old.

In my half-drowsy state, I walked woodenly behind her, knowing some terrible calamity had taken place but not sure yet what it would mean to my already fractured world. In the living room stood five or six men and women, all strangers to me. We had not even had a chance to attend the small branch, yet here were members of the Church to help my mother at this terrible moment. We all stood in a circle, and someone was saying we needed to pray. At some point, the enormity of it settled in, and tears started to fall. A woman put her arm around me and held me close.

The next morning, Mother expected Sara and me to go to school. Looking back, she probably needed us to be cared for while she dealt with a hundred details, but I didn't see how I could. I asked her to at least write a note to the teacher. I couldn't just go to school as if the world had not irrevocably changed overnight. So Mother scribbled a note. I took the note to school and, with great self-control, handed it to my teacher. She began walking away then stopped, turned, and read the note to the class. She looked at my stiffly composed face and said, "Aren't you sad?" The dam broke, and I put my head down on my desk and cried and cried.

We headed back to Seattle for the funeral, and the procession that followed us to the cemetery was more than a mile long. But everything we owned was still in Illinois, and a week later we headed back.

Once home, we tried to pick up the reins of life. It was not easy. My mother was forty-two and had been a full-time homemaker who had created a home for a husband and six children. She had two years of college behind her and no real marketable skills. Those first weeks were very hard. There was no money coming in. In time, she applied for and received Social Security survivors' benefits and found a low-paying job that would get us through. But right then, those first weeks, we were in great financial distress.

Our sister Carol went to work instead of to college, and my brother Doug took up an offer to live with an aunt and uncle in Oregon to finish high school there. I felt like our whole family was somehow falling apart. Sara and I came home from school to an empty home, something we had never had to do before. It was a sad time.

One Saturday morning, my mother changed out of her clean-the-house dress and into a nice go-to-the-store dress, as women did in those days. She picked up her handbag and then, instead of leaving to do the grocery shopping as she had done for countless years, she went into the living room and sat on the sofa.

Curious, I went to sit by her and asked what she was doing.

She responded, "I am waiting to get some money so I can do my grocery shopping. I have been a faithful tithe payer all my life. Today I am waiting for the Lord to provide a way for me to buy groceries."

This struck me with great wonderment. I continued to sit and wait with her. I wanted to know what could possibly happen to provide us with grocery money—right then. A few minutes later, the doorbell rang. I could hardly believe it, and I ran to answer it. A man stood there. He inquired if we had any suits belonging to my father that he could buy.

Mother recognized him and invited him in. He had been over a few days earlier after finding out we had some men's clothing in his size. He was of a similar size to my father: short and round. The man then explained that he had been paid *that very day*, unexpectedly, by his employer, who usually waited until the end of the month. He wondered if we had any more suits he could buy. We did, and a bargain was struck. The man left very pleased to have found additional clothing in his size.

Mother picked up her handbag and told us she now had the *exact* amount of money she generally spent at the grocery store, and she left to go shopping.

I was deeply impressed as a child, both by my mother's faith and by the immediate result. It was a lesson that stayed with me.

The following summer my mother moved us all to Provo, Utah, where she entered Brigham Young University on a scholarship and eventually earned a master's degree in social work. She was able to provide for our family from then on and even supported a son and a daughter on a mission and all of us through college.

Fast forward ten years. I was a college student out on my own. I shared an apartment with a working girl who was not a student, so we didn't live in student housing. The apartment had been rented in my name, so even though we shared costs, I was ultimately responsible for the rent. After a couple months, my roommate decided to move out, and I was faced with having to pay the entire rent by myself. I was twenty years old at the time and a junior in college. About then I decided to serve a mission and put in my papers, but I needed additional income to sustain me in the apartment for at least three or four months.

As I searched for some kind of part-time job, I stumbled upon the Fuller Brush company. At that time it was a popular household brand sold door-to-door by Fuller Brush salesmen. There were few women selling it, but I wanted to give it a try and signed up.

I received my sample case and found out that it would be at least two weeks between sending in the orders, getting the products back, and collecting my money. Still, it was the only job I could find that fit in with my part-time job as a receptionist in a car wash and my class schedule at the university.

One Friday, I received my check from my job at the car wash, and on Sunday I intended to pay my tithing. But as I did the math, I realized I could either pay a full tithing now, or I could pay the rent in full a week later when it fell due—but not both. I was alone with no one to help me, and I didn't know how to get the money for the rent if I went ahead and paid my tithing as usual.

As I stood in the meetinghouse foyer undecided, I thought back to my mother's example. The blessings that came into our home that Saturday morning years ago could not be easily dismissed. So I simply decided to pay my tithing. I did not know what to do about the rent, but in the end, I could not walk out of church without giving that envelope to the bishop.

The next day, after work and classes, I started on my first block of knocking on doors to sell hairbrushes and cleaning products. Nearly every home I went to invited me in and placed an order. Not only that, but they also all paid me on the spot. By Saturday, a week later, I had earned enough to pay the company for the products and had my profit as well. It was just enough to pay my full rent on time!

As wonderful as this was, there was yet one more lesson I learned from this experience. I continued to sell Fuller Brush products right up to the time I left on my mission, and never again did a single customer pay me up front. Not once. That's when I realized the Lord had really opened that door for me. It wasn't luck or just my hard work. The Lord had created such good feelings in each home I visited that first week on the job that every single customer trusted me, a complete stranger, to take their money first and return with their orders later.

The Lord had given me a testimony of the blessings of paying a full tithing first before worrying about worldly debts. I knew I had been blessed to earn all I needed that week and only the Lord could have opened that door.

This blessing of having the faith to keep this particular commandment had its start when I was only a child of ten, as I watched and learned from my mother's example. And it came full-circle in my life as I experienced my own moment of choice as a young woman when faced with a difficult adult decision that could bring some unpleasant consequences. This faith to do the right thing led to a strong testimony of tithing that has served me all my life.

Judy C. Olsen has been writing and editing for the LDS audience for many years. She and her husband, Don, live in Sandy, Utah, and are parents of four children and grandparents of sixteen grandchildren. Judy enjoys writing, sewing, and crafts.

They who have faith in him will cleave unto every good thing;
wherefore he advocateth the cause of the children of men.

—Moroni 7:28

A Toast to the Russians

By Stephen Thelin

In 1986 I was in the Air Force serving in the Titan program office at Los Angeles Air Force Base. Though only in my late twenties, I had the responsibility for Titan launches at Cape Canaveral and was deeply involved in important national security efforts.

Nevertheless, I made a decision to leave the air force because of concerns for my family life. After leaving the air force, we moved to the state of Washington, where I had been offered a job by the Boeing Space and Defense Group to work on a classified program dealing with the Air Force.

Because of my launch experience, I was asked to help develop a new program called Sea Launch, where we launched satellites into orbit from the middle of the ocean. It was a commercial venture using Ukrainian rockets, Russian upper stages, Norwegian ships, and American payloads and support operations. The program started as a request from the state department to explore any ideas we might have that could leverage the extensive space capabilities of the former USSR countries, help employ some of their rocket scientists for peaceful purposes, and help get their economy going.

Sea Launch wound up being a wonderful example of beating swords into plowshares, and we felt a real sense of purpose and delight in working with our former adversaries. I started as an engineer, but I eventually wound up as mission director, responsible for all ship and launch vehicle operations to get commercial satellites, such as Direct TV, XM Radio, PanAmSat (supporting the 2000 Olympics), and other similar projects into orbit.

As the mission director, I was ever conscious of setting a good example of what a Latter-day Saint father, husband, and mission director should be. I looked for opportunities to strengthen others and their convictions regarding Latter-day Saints. For example, I was able to arrange nondenominational church services onboard the command ship, although there were only three Latter-day Saints on board. I was a bishop at the time and usually conducted the services.

I also found a way to bring onboard more Latter-day Saints. Communication was always a challenge with our Russian counterparts. Since I needed Russian-speaking engineers who also spoke English, I went on a recruiting trip to Utah. I asked to interview all engineering students who had served a mission in Russia, and I ended up interviewing thirteen students at Brigham Young University, University of Utah, and Utah State University. I hired three, and they made a big difference in helping our relationships with the Russians and Ukrainians.

These small efforts at fostering good feelings toward the Church were fine, but I soon found out a larger challenge awaited. As we continued to develop both personal and professional relationships (just a couple years after the dissolution of the USSR), we took a number of trips to both Russia and Ukraine.

During one of my first trips to Moscow, I was the head of the Boeing/U.S. delegation. At the end of our visit, the Russians hosted a party honoring us and all we had accomplished throughout the previous two and a half weeks. Everyone stood up, glasses in hand. Suddenly, I realized they expected us to drink a toast with them and that I was expected to give the first toast. What to do? We could not afford to offend our hosts, and my job demanded I do *whatever necessary* to maintain good relations with our Russian colleagues.

I quickly looked around. There was nothing available to drink that was nonalcoholic, not even water, and I had no time to find anything. Everyone was waiting.

I could have just put the glass to my lips, but I didn't want them to think I would drink just because it was a special occasion. So with my heart hammering, I picked up a piece of chocolate candy. I told them that I hoped this would not offend them but that my religious beliefs did not allow me to drink alcoholic beverages. Then I gave a big flowery toast, said cheers, and took a bite. It was very quiet in the room. The men looked quizzically at each other, even after the translation, but finally they shrugged their shoulders and took a drink. I worried what might come of the event.

Instead of censure, I gained a level of respect I did not have before. A few months later, we were in Ukraine at one of the Cold War rocket plants when they held another party, and again, toasting was required. This time, I got some water to put into my vodka glass. But as I did so, one of the Ukrainians came running up to me saying, "*Nyet, nyet, nyet!*" (no, no, no). He replaced my vodka glass with a water glass. Because of the stand I had taken before, he knew I didn't have vodka in my glass, and he wanted to make sure everyone else knew I was drinking only water.

From that time on, whenever I visited Russia, or, later on, while onboard the ships during mission operations, my Russian counterparts always had sparkling cider or a similar beverage for me. And when they visited in the United States, I often invited many of them over to our house for dinner, especially after my wife, Ki'i, learned to speak Russian. These men I worked with loved both of us, and we developed a very special relationship with the Russians and Ukrainians. I was even able to give the Book of Mormon to some of the men.

One day I invited some visiting senior Russian leaders to dinner at our house. After dinner, we started to talk about religion and what my responsibilities were at church (bishop of the Lake Wilderness ward in the Maple Valley, Washington, stake). I took them over to our stake center for a tour. We spent more than two hours walking through the building, as their curiosity and questions allowed us to talk about every aspect of the Church. I found that the selection of pictures and paintings in the building provided me with an opportunity to discuss virtually all of the Church doctrines.

One senior-level dignitary later told me he had been to the United States nineteen times and had visited many places—including Disney World; Cape Canaveral; Washington, DC; and other landmarks—but the tour of our humble stake center was the most interesting thing he had ever done in the U.S.

I'm grateful for the opportunities I've had to share our Latter-day Saint beliefs in seemingly small but meaningful ways. Living true to our standards has always brought respect, even in delicate situations. I love the Lord and have been grateful for the opportunity to set an example for my Russian and Ukrainian friends, as well as many others, of what a Latter-day Saint should be.

Steve and his wife, Ki'i, live in Tucson, Arizona. Their five children are grown, and they have seven grandchildren. Steve serves on the high council in the Sahuarita, Arizona, Stake. He works for Raytheon as chief engineer, developing new missiles for President Obama's missile defense approach (fourth phase of his phase-adaptive approach to be fielded in 2020).

Wherefore teach it unto your children, that all men, everywhere, must repent, or they can in nowise inherit the kingdom of God.

—Moses 6:57

Listening to Dougie

By Sara Hacken

When my son Douglas was just two years old, he begged for a pet. Because we lived in a small apartment, I decided the only pet we could manage would be a bird—preferably a canary. So off we went to the pet store, where Dougie immediately spotted a little yellow canary singing away in his cage. This seemed like the perfect pet, so we bought the bird on the spot and brought him home.

We put the bird cage on the counter between the living room and the kitchen so we could better see and hear our new little pet. Dougie loved his little canary and named him Happy Bird because of the cheerful song we often heard wafting over the bustle of our family's activities.

As a proper pet owner, I cleaned the bird cage on a regular schedule, sometimes with a little help from Dougie. One day, because I was in a hurry, I took care of the bird without alerting Dougie. I quickly cleaned out the cage, put clean paper on the bottom tray, filled the food and water cups, and put the cage gently back on the ledge. But Dougie saw what I was doing and wanted to help—as always. I was already finished and hurrying to get out the door. Much to my dismay, as he reached for the cage, Dougie accidentally bumped it, and the cage flew off the counter and onto the floor.

Annoyance coursed through me. The bird was flying around hysterically, water and birdseed covered the carpet in a wet mess, and now Dougie was crying. Why, when I was in such a hurry, did this have to happen? Hot words rose to my tongue.

As I opened my mouth to vent my irritation, a very clear impression came into my mind: *Let him repent.*

I was so taken aback that I stopped in my tracks, and the angry words died in my throat. Let him *repent*? How does a two-year old repent? How could a two-year old make restitution?

I quickly thought about it, and then with great patience, I let Dougie pick up the cage and helped him put it back on the counter. We quietly put more water and birdseed into the cups, soothed the poor little bird, and got a towel to blot the water and the vacuum cleaner to clean the mess on the carpet. Suddenly, I wasn't in such a hurry anymore. I was teaching my son how to correct a mistake, something I had not given much thought to before. Of course a small child does not need to repent, but all children need to learn the process of how to right a wrong when they make a mistake, or how else might they understand the steps of repentance later on?

I could not have known how very important this experience would be for Dougie—and for me. At that time, I operated a daycare center in my home to help bring in some much-needed grad-student income, and several young children came daily to our busy house, where I cared for them, taught them, read stories to them, and played with them.

Two weeks before Dougie's third birthday, he started to run a fever. I wasn't overly concerned since he occasionally had ear infections, the flu, and once even had a good case of chicken pox. I gave him a cool bath, some children's aspirin, and put him to bed.

The following morning, I found my son lying unconscious in his bed with blood spattered all over his pillow (I found out later he had bit his tongue). I called the doctor, who lived close by, and she immediately came over, took one look at him, and called the hospital. We rushed him to the emergency room, where they were waiting for him. They immediately started him on several medications, and I thought all would be well. But he passed away from meningitis just twenty-four hours later. I was alone with him when he died. He never regained consciousness, and I was never able to say good-bye to him. I longed to cuddle him and tell him one more time how much I loved him, but it was not possible.

At the same time, one of the children from my daycare also came down with meningitis, but a different strain, and he recovered with no ill effects. With great effort, I went to see him in the same hospital where my little boy had died.

Our ward family gathered around to help us. Ward members did our laundry and brought us meals. One close friend volunteered to make a coffin for Dougie, and several Relief Society sisters upholstered the coffin in blue satin, complete with a hand-embroidered pillow. Another member had a brand new black station wagon and offered to take Dougie's little coffin to the cemetery.

I dreaded his funeral because I knew I would be an emotional mess—my feelings are never far from the surface anyway. So I tried hard to keep my feelings in check and to not look at that tiny casket. We honored him with his favorite song, "Give Said the Little Stream," then a poem about his life, then a talk by the bishop. A sad trip to the cemetery followed and, finally, the dedication of his small grave. I had worked hard to stay composed through all of it, and then it was over at last.

It was at the family dinner after the funeral that I learned another important lesson. All of my brothers and sisters had made a great effort to be with me, some even driving all night to come. My oldest sister, Pat, drew me aside after the dinner and said, "Sara, I have a message for you from Dougie."

I was shocked. A message for me?

"Dougie tried to get through to you during the funeral, but your mind was too busy. He wanted to tell you that he loved you and that he was okay."

Then I broke down and wept. Oh, how I had wanted to hear his voice one more time! To find out that he had tried to communicate with me was sweet, but that he couldn't get through because my mind was too busy was a terrible revelation.

Shortly after Dougie's death, Happy Bird suddenly died too. It felt for a time that all of the sunshine had gone out of my life. I wondered if Happy Bird had gone to be with Dougie. While I didn't know, it helped to think of my son there with his little pet.

However, as difficult as this time was, I often became aware of the Spirit present in my home, bringing sweet, peaceful comfort that helped me understand that I could go on, that death was not the end, and that Father in Heaven knew and understood my feelings.

Many times, I have thought back to my son's experience in upsetting the birdcage. What I thought was just a significant lesson in good parenting that I had received that day suddenly took on a deeper, more eternal meaning. My son had been given an opportunity to reveal his tender heart, make what effort a small child could to repent, and show a willingness to keep the commandments in this small but now very important way. And I had helped him, thanks to a gracious and understanding Father who knew what was to come. I have always treasured that eternal lesson in patience and motherhood, and I have been so grateful for that teaching moment with my son.

Even though I had not said good-bye to him in the way my heart desired, he had found a way to say *I love you* to me, for which I have always been grateful. He too must have longed for the very same thing: to share words of love one last time.

I also understood from these experiences how important it is to listen to the whisperings of the Spirit all of the time, especially when we are hurt, angry, or sad. There are important lessons to be learned if we will listen and obey, such as eternal gospel lessons for a two-year-old as well as eternal lessons in parenting—if we will just receive them.

Sara Hacken is a teacher in the gifted and talented programs of the Alpine School District. She lives in Orem, Utah, where she is active in her community and spends time with her children and grandchildren.

Yea, behold, I will tell you in your mind and
in your heart, by the Holy Ghost, which shall come
upon you and which shall dwell in your heart.

—D&C 8:2

Go Back First

By Judy Young

My husband, Rocky, and I lived in Logan, Utah, while he attended Utah State University. During the summer of 1971, my husband worked for the Wonder Bread company, making deliveries to outlying towns. His route was so spread out that sometimes he had to spend a night or two on the road.

We had a baby who was just about six months old, and I was a full-time homemaker who stayed pretty close to home all the time. In fact, in our short married life, we had never even spent a night together in a motel. I thought it would be fun to accompany my husband sometime but not with a very young baby.

Then my mother, who lived in Evanston, Wyoming, which was a little more than an hour away to the east, offered to watch our daughter while I drove to Montpelier, Idaho, to stay overnight with Rocky. It sounded like a great adventure, and I accepted. I drove to Evanston and dropped off the baby then headed north to Montpelier. My husband and I had a fun visit together. The next morning, I left first and headed back to Evanston to pick up our daughter. Rocky left soon after I did, traveling toward Logan.

I was nearly to Garden City—about twenty miles into my drive to Evanston—when I heard an announcement on the radio. A delivery van had crashed into a car on a bridge just outside of Montpelier. A delivery van? In that instant, I knew it was Rocky who had crashed—the kind of knowing that only comes through the Spirit. I wanted to turn around right then and go to him, but I felt very clearly that I should go back *first* to Evanston and pick up both my mother and my baby and then head for Logan.

I was shocked, but I listened and kept going toward Evanston. I had many questions and many worries about my husband. Nevertheless, I rushed on, not knowing that Rocky had already asked the highway patrol to find me so I could come back. Needless to say, no one caught up with me.

All the way to Evanston, I kept worrying. *How would they find me or get ahold of me if he were unconscious or so badly injured that he couldn't tell them where I had gone?* In the middle of my worries, a spirit of calm distilled upon me, and I was at peace. For one thing, my father worked at the fire hall and knew all the policemen and highway patrolmen. If they couldn't find me, I was sure they would call my dad.

As soon as I walked into my parents' home, I asked Dad if anyone had called. I was white and shaken, and they asked what had happened. I told them I thought Rocky had been in a car wreck. Dad just laughed and told me not to worry; he was sure it wasn't Rocky.

I had only been in the house a few minutes when the phone rang. Dad answered then handed it to me. It was the highway patrol, letting me know that Rocky's van had hit a car that had stopped suddenly in front of him. He had seriously injured his leg, and they were taking him by ambulance to the hospital in Logan. I asked the officer to tell Rocky I would see him soon.

My mother came with me and my daughter as we returned to our home in Logan. I went straight to the hospital. Because of a broken femur, they had to build a special rod to put inside Rocky's bone. As things turned out, I spent the next nine days at the hospital. Mom stayed with my sweet baby at our home, fixed our meals, and kept things clean. Her help was invaluable.

If I had reacted as I first wanted to do that day by turning back to go to my husband's aid, I would have ended up in Logan without my mother's help and the company of my daughter. My parents only owned one car, and my father needed it to go to work, so my mother could not have come to help me. By listening to the Spirit, I was blessed with my mother's company and support at a time I deeply needed both. I was very grateful for the strong feelings that entered my heart and guided me to get my daughter first. I know the Lord was watching out for the welfare of all of us on that very stressful occasion.

Judy Young and her husband, Rocky, have been married for forty-one years, with thirty-eight of those years spent in Evanston, Wyoming. Parents of ten, they have seven living children, one daughter in heaven, two special-needs adopted children, and twenty-five grandchildren. They have also fostered more than fifty children. Judy was employed for many years in the school district's special education program, where today she still works as a substitute teacher.

Let your hearts be full, drawn out in prayer
unto him continually for your welfare, and also for
the welfare of those who are around you.

—Alma 34:27

The Storm

By Gloria Martinez

My husband and I traveled from our home in Sacramento, California, to Mesa, Arizona, to visit our son and his wife, see their newest baby, and attend the baby blessing. The visit seemed all too short. As we prepared to leave Mesa for home, it began to rain pretty hard. We usually begin every trip with a prayer, asking for the Lord's watchful care, and this time was no different.

Hours on the road went by, and we crossed into California toward home. It continued to rain all day. We planned to stay the night in the Los Angeles area, and as we approached from the south, we decided to drive on through the large metropolitan area to the north end so we would have a shorter trip home the next day. As we drove along, we considered various routes, including swinging north through Pasadena and hitting Interstate 5 from that direction. But we had never driven that route and didn't know how heavy the traffic on the freeway might be or if it really saved any time. We decided to stay on I-10 into downtown Los Angeles, meet Interstate 5, and then head north on I-5.

It began to get dark. It got harder to see and drive in the rain. In fact, the rain came down so hard that water flooded the road and splashed onto the windshield with every passing car. Lights reflected off the wet road, vehicles—everything—and it was hard to see the lane markings and keep track of traffic. At times, the car would hydroplane. We wondered if we should just stop and wait until morning. But if we stopped now, we'd have the morning rush-hour traffic to fight heading right into the city center. So we decided to try to push on as planned.

Because it's difficult to find radio stations we both enjoy listening to while traveling, we seldom turn on the radio. Instead, we generally bring our own tapes or CDs. On this night, however, for some unknown reason, John simply reached over and turned on the radio. We *never* do that! He pushed all the buttons, trying to find a news program. Just as he tuned in to one station, he heard what sounded like a report on local road conditions. Some roads were closed and a couple of the interstate highway interchanges were closed. Much to our shock, we heard that the I-10 to I-5 interchange was one of them—the very one we were headed for! Perhaps there had been a bad accident.

We suddenly realized we needed to change our plan, so we got out our map to see where the turnoff to Pasadena was—if we had not already passed it. We squinted through the heavy rain, trying to read the upcoming exit signs and were relieved to see it just a few miles down the road. We easily swung onto the other freeway and went up around Pasadena. We continued on to our I-5 interchange. We were so tired and stressed by then that we had to stop. We took an exit, at last, and found a motel in the area.

We got to our room, deeply grateful to be out of the storm, the dark, the confusing lights reflecting everywhere, and the stress. To relax, we turned on the TV to a news channel. To our shock and amazement, the newscast showed massive flooding in downtown Los Angeles. The streets had become rivers, and several cars were nearly submerged. The very freeway we would have been on and the cities we would have had to pass through were completely under water.

There's no doubt in our minds the Lord prompted John to turn on the radio at the *exact time* they were announcing the freeway interchange was closed—and just in time to be able to turn off and go around it all! If we had continued into Los Angeles, we likely would have been shunted off onto other roads, and it would probably have taken us many hours to find our way through unfamiliar streets to get to safety.

I have thought of how the Lord warns us "betimes" in scriptural language, meaning "in time" or with time to prepare (see Job 8:5 or Proverb 13:24). Turning on the radio right then gave us our own warning "betimes," just in time to take a safer route. We were so glad we'd said a prayer and asked the Lord to *protect* and *guide* us. Simple words, really, and often spoken in prayer, but on this day, they came to have deep meaning for us. The Lord did guide us and keep us from danger, and we were very grateful.

Gloria Martinez lives in Layton, Utah, with her husband, John. They are the parents of nine children and grandparents of thirty-three grandchildren and fifteen great-grandchildren. They currently serve in the offices of the Perpetual Education Fund in Salt Lake City.

And God Did Hear Our Cries
and Did Answer Our Prayers

—Mosiah 9:18

But this is not all; they had given themselves
to much prayer, and fasting; therefore they had
the spirit of prophecy, and the spirit of revelation.

—Alma 17:3

The Power of Family Fasting and Prayer

By Ki'inani (Debi) Thelin

I met my husband, Steve, in a drivers' training class in high school in Southern California, and we eventually married and started our family. He was serving in the air force, and he'd decided to make a career of it. But his assignments with the Titan missile program took him more and more often away from home.

One day I had gone to the park with our children. Our three-year-old son, Nick, spotted an airplane in the sky. He pointed and said, "There goes Daddy." Nick thought his father lived on an airplane! I recounted the incident to Steve, and he was shocked. Nick began to say this even when Steve was home. This made us start thinking and evaluating our life and priorities.

Over the next two years, Steve continued to work extremely long hours with extensive travel, sometimes to Cocoa Beach (Cape Canaveral), Florida, for up to thirty days at a time. To compound this, we had five children and couldn't fit into any of the base housing units, so we had no choice but to live in Riverside, the only place we could afford to buy a house on a lieutenant's pay. The commute was sixty-three miles one way through some of the worst traffic in the world, so Steve often left at 4:30 a.m. and was gone from home most of the day.

He began to seriously question where he was headed with his life. Was he spending enough time as a parent? As a husband? Should he change careers? Leave the air force? His work was very important to our country, and he felt a deep obligation to see it through. In addition, since he had not worked in the private sector before, just the idea of leaving the air force was a little scary. Plus, he only had nine years to a full military retirement.

Unsure of what to do, we decided to take it to the Lord as a family and then follow His direction, whatever it was. We started fasting and praying every Sunday, not just on fast Sunday. After months of fasting, we started to get some answers. Our first clear understanding came that, yes, it was time to leave the air force. So Steve started sending out résumés, and before long, he had six or seven good offers in several different cities. Where should we go?

We continued to fast and pray as a family, and soon we felt our answer was to move to Seattle. The trouble was, Steve had interviewed with Boeing Aircraft, but we did not have an offer from the company, nor were we sure we were going to get one. So we continued to fast and pray. But the feeling persisted. We eventually knew without a doubt that we needed to move to Seattle, so we went ahead and ordered the moving truck then proceeded on faith.

It was a nerve-wracking time because we didn't even know what part of the greater Seattle metropolitan area—which stretches about a hundred miles, from Canada practically to the Oregon line—to move to or what Steve would be doing to support our family once we arrived, but we proceeded as we felt directed. The day arrived when the moving van came to pack our belongings. Just as the van started pulling away, the mail came—and with it, an offer for employment with Boeing Aircraft at the Kent facility, south of Seattle! Having an offer in hand was a great relief, but at the same time, it was not entirely surprising because of the strong answers to our prayers we had received during the past weeks. The whole family knew it was right.

Since we had received so much inspiration regarding the move, we continued to fast and pray as a family every Sunday, not only to thank the Lord for so many blessings but also to find out if there was a particular place He wanted us to live. First, we settled into a rental home in Kent; then we began looking around and getting to know the area. We had a feeling we should explore a place called Maple Valley, which was out in the country. We even attended church there. Instantly, we felt like we were home.

We started fasting once again, this time praying about whether to buy a particular piece of property. One Sunday, while we were still fasting, we drove out to this property after church to see how we felt about it. We had each of the children say a prayer, then I offered a heartfelt prayer, and then Steve prayed.

I felt a great sense of peace. Steve told me that when he opened his eyes, he had the most wonderful feeling come over him. The Spirit in the car was the strongest I had ever felt. Most of us had tears in our eyes, and we felt like we knew how Brigham Young must have felt when he declared, "This is the place."

We had worried if this out-of-the-way property would be a good investment or not, but because of the good feelings we'd experienced, we proceeded with the purchase of three acres and began making plans to build our new home. In time, we built a beautiful home and raised our five children in it. It turned out to be a sound investment for our children's sake and for our financial well-being.

The bishop of our ward, Bishop Reese, built his home on the lot next to ours, and he helped us during the construction phase. Later, as more Latter-day Saints moved into that area, Steve was called to be the bishop of a new ward.

It took about six months of weekly fasts, lots of prayers, and a little bit of faith on our part, but we all grew closer to the Lord through this experience, especially the children. They learned firsthand how to solve problems and how to approach God for answers. I thank Heavenly Father for the direction and help He gave us in moving from the hectic life we had been leading in Los Angeles to our beautiful home nestled in the woods of the Northwest, where we could turn our attention to teaching the precious spirits He had entrusted us with and serving in the Church.

Ki'inani Thelin has been dancing hula and Polynesian dances since she was a small child. She has performed professionally wherever she's lived, including the Marshall Islands and Hawaii. Ki'inani currently teaches hula and Polynesian dance classes at a studio in Arizona. She also enjoys choreography, designing and sewing Polynesian costumes, making jewelry, creating her own Hawaiian-style clothing line, scrapbooking, reading, scuba diving, traveling, and spending time with her best friend (her husband, Steve), her five children, and her seven grandchildren. She loves to spread the "Aloha Spirit" as well as the Spirit of our Heavenly Father every chance she gets.

Come unto me, all ye that labour and are
heavy laden, and I will give you rest. Take my yoke
upon you, and learn of me; for I am meek and lowly in heart:
and ye shall find rest unto your souls. For my yoke
is easy, and my burden is light.

—Matthew 11:28–30

Encircled by Light

By Susanne C. Morley

Shortly after I was married, I got a job at an insurance company. The office where I worked was a long drive from where I lived. It was wintertime, and the roads were sometimes slick or hazardous. Despite the weather and distance, I don't believe I was ever late getting to work.

My main responsibility was to type up stacks of complicated paperwork on an old-fashioned typewriter. Only the bosses had computers. I worked hard at the job, but it was very involved, and I often wondered whether I was working as fast as they hoped.

My main concern came from a supervisor, a young woman who seemed to have it in for me. If papers were missing or filed improperly, she assumed I had made the mistake. I was feeling a lot of stress.

To make matters worse, another employee seemed nice, but she had a strange accent that was hard to understand. Try as I would, I had trouble taking direction and learning my duties from her. I must admit, I was naive and unsure of myself at the time, which didn't help the situation.

If all this wasn't enough, there was yet another sore spot that troubled the company boss. I didn't want to sign up for their insurance plan because I was already insured through my husband's work. Whether it was true or not, I became convinced that my refusal to participate became an issue with a few of my fellow coworkers, people I thought ought to be my friends but for some reason weren't. A feeling began to grow in my heart that they didn't want to come right out and fire me, but they wanted me to quit. This made working there a misery.

I dreaded coming to work, and I spent my days living in fear of criticism. The young supervisor was especially impatient and mean. I was so anxious while I was at work that I was physically ill part of the time. I even spent time in the restroom nauseated and vomiting.

One day, I was so miserable with this state of affairs that I went into the restroom, knelt down on the floor, and prayed for relief. The constant cold shoulders, criticisms, pointed looks, and seeming disapproval were more than I could stand.

I poured out my heart to Heavenly Father, asking for help. What could I do? Was there any way to fix this? How could I move forward? How could I even go back to my desk today? I ended the prayer, and as I arose to my feet, I immediately began to feel better. My stomach didn't hurt. I could sense warmth and comfort surround me and fill me. My heart was at peace. In fact, as I walked back to my desk and the job at hand, I felt like I was encircled by a warm, comforting light. I could almost see this light and wondered if anyone else could.

It was soon clear that no one else was aware of the change within me. The supervisor was just as mean and rude as ever, but suddenly her attitude didn't bother me in the least. Nothing anyone said or did bothered me at all. I went about my work peacefully, as though they didn't exist. The healing of my heart and soul was complete.

This peace sustained me for a period of time. It became clear, however, that I had to make a change, so I decided to quit that job, knowing I could get one with a kinder environment somewhere else.

I have thought much about this answer to a plea from a young woman who felt friendless and suffered so much stress from workplace meanness. I appreciated the healing the Lord blessed me with, enabling me to continue on with my work that day.

Susanne Morley is a mother and grandmother. She lives in West Valley City, Utah. A longtime member of the League of Utah Writers, Oquirrh Writers' chapter, she enjoys entering writing contests and meeting with the chapter group to critique and exchange ideas. She also works as an editor and ghostwriter.

The Lord hath been mindful of us: he will bless us.

—Psalms 115:12

Butterfly Help

By Donna Marley

As we awaited the birth of our son, we were anxious to find out if he was going to have hemophilia like his grandfather Gordon Murray Thelin. Hemophilia is a condition with which the body does not make a clotting factor to stop bleeding. Of course I was worried about the normal cuts and bruises of raising a young child with this condition. But even more troubling was the fact that hemophiliacs also bleed inside, where it can't be seen until pain makes it known—usually in the joints and muscles, such as knees and elbows.

As a daughter of a hemophiliac, I had about a fifty-fifty chance of passing this condition on to my son. When Cameron was born, he tested positive. I had seen the suffering of my father, who passed away in his late thirties, so I had some idea of what this was going to mean in our own lives. But I also had hope.

You see, my father, a biochemist, devoted his life to the study of hematology in an effort to help those who suffered from hemophilia. Just before he passed away, he made a breakthrough discovery. He isolated the missing factor in the blood and created a clotting treatment. The treatment was soon made available to the public, easing some of the pain, problems, and suffering of thousands of people. This clotting factor, usually just referred to as *factor*, would also help my son.

The treatment had to be administered by IV directly into the bloodstream. When my son was small, my husband and I would work together to give him the treatments: one would hold him and comfort him while the other gave the infusion. He often cried, and it broke our hearts to have to poke him with the butterfly-tipped needle. However, if we didn't give it to him, we knew he would be subject to tremendous pain for weeks, causing permanent damage to the affected joints and muscles. So we tried to learn how to make the butterfly needle hit a good vein on the first try.

We watched our son grow, carefully monitoring his activities. We wanted him to live as normally as possible, but we had to take care. Activities like jumping off a swing or roughhousing with his siblings would likely start an internal bleed, but through faith and prayers, and with factor close by, we let him be a boy first and a hemophiliac second.

We carried factor everywhere we went. Everywhere. We never left home without a small cooler holding the precious treatment.

One day when Cameron was about two years old, he began hemorrhaging in his ankle while my mother-in-law was visiting. I went for the factor and explained to him that he needed an infusion. He had become used to this, but Daddy wasn't home to hold him. Normally, Cameron would sit on Dad's lap for comfort while Mommy started the IV. But this time, his grandma pulled him onto her lap. He kept calling for his daddy and did not want to start without him. He became distressed. His muscles tensed, and the needle would not penetrate the vein.

I tried several times to hit a vein, but he was too tense, and the vein would just roll. After three tries and a lot of fishing for a vein, Cameron had had enough, and his ankle was becoming more painful. I was beginning to despair.

Finally, I put down the needle and said, "Cameron, let's have a prayer and ask Heavenly Father to help us find a vein."

So we bowed our heads and asked for help.

As we opened our eyes, a butterfly fluttered to the window and settled on the ledge. It immediately caught Cameron's attention, and for the next few minutes, he sat spellbound, watching the beautiful butterfly as it moved and fluttered. He laughed with delight as the butterfly entertained him, and the tension melted away.

I was able to quickly find a vein and infuse the lifesaving treatment into my son's body. As I finished, the butterfly opened its wings and fluttered away.

The Lord has many ways to answer prayers, and I was grateful that He would provide a colorful butterfly for a little boy who needed some help that day.

Donna Marley and her husband, Doug, are parents of eleven, eight of whom were adopted through the foster-adopt program for children with special needs. They live on Camano Island, just outside Seattle, Washington.

And we know that all things work together for good to them that love God, to them who are the called according to his purpose.

—Romans 8:28

An Unforgettable Witness

By Gina Lynn Shelley

There was never a doubt in my mind that one day I would serve a mission. Ever since I was a young girl in Primary, I wanted to be a missionary. In fact, the song "I Hope They Call Me on a Mission" was my all-time favorite, and I asked to sing it every week. In junior high school, my desire to be a missionary persisted, and I began sharing the gospel with my neighborhood friends, which resulted in the conversion of my friend, her mother, and her little sister. High school was no different. I took to heart that "every member is a missionary," and I always looked for opportunities to share the gospel. I even had a couple of friends get baptized. When I received my patriarchal blessing, it confirmed that I was to be a missionary, and I quietly rejoiced and looked forward with even more anticipation to serving a mission.

I soon found myself a freshman attending Brigham Young University and living in the dorms. All the young men in my freshmen ward were preparing to leave on their missions after a semester or two of school, and I couldn't wait until it was my turn to go. Yet, as much as I wanted to be a missionary, I also looked forward to one day falling in love and getting married. I was also aware of the Brethren's advice in this area, that a woman should consider marriage over a mission if the choice came to that.

In the fall of my freshman year, I did meet someone—Nick. He seemed to be a perfect fit for me in every way. We fell head over heels for each other. His mother had just recently gone through a divorce, and the family he had grown up with had suddenly been torn apart. Nick was alone at BYU while preparing to serve a mission in January. He left me with a promise ring, and I was prepared to wait. I sent him off, promising to write. Since he would be returning home just about the time I would turn twenty-one—the age sisters are allowed to serve a mission—my desires of going on a mission were now being pushed further and further back with each passing month.

The following summer, while working at Aspen Grove, I met a returned missionary named Chris. I felt pulled to this new young man. Shortly after summer ended, our relationship became very serious. I felt I needed to be with him, but my feelings were not the same as they had been for Nick. In my prayers, I pleaded for direction and help to know what to do.

I was torn three different ways. I felt that if I continued dating Chris, he would probably propose. Yet I had feelings for Nick and part of me wanted to wait until he came home from his mission before I made a decision. And what about my patriarchal blessing and my longing to serve a mission?

I knew I had to take some painful steps. They began with writing a "Dear John" to Nick. I wasn't being fair to him—or to Chris. I had to choose. And I continued to feel that my future lay with Chris, so I trusted my feelings and followed them. Chris and I were soon engaged. He gave me a ring, and I thought everything was figured out. As it turned out, I was wrong.

All summer long, Chris complained of a pain in his knee. It had progressively gotten worse, so he finally went to a doctor. Chris was unprepared to find out he had bone cancer. Cancer! He was only twenty-three years old! How could this happen?

How was this going to affect our relationship and marriage? How far had it spread? Would he even survive? Should we go ahead and marry? His home was in California, but should he continue on at BYU?

We didn't have the answers to these questions, so we began to pray more fervently about what to do. I continued to feel I needed to stay with him. Months passed, filled with heartfelt prayers for his recovery, for guidance, and for help. Chris continued his studies, hoping for the best. To our sorrow, chemotherapy was not working, and the day came when his doctor told him he would have to amputate his leg in order to prevent the cancer from spreading further.

After the painful surgery, Chris and I had a long talk. He told me he had much to work through and would be living at home in California permanently. He was not in a position to get married and wouldn't be for some time. Deep inside, I knew it was the right decision. I returned the ring.

But still, it hurt. I had felt so strongly I needed to be with him. Why was that? After more prayers, I finally came to understand that my time with Chris had been meant mainly to sustain and help him through a difficult and challenging time—not to marry him, as I had assumed.

Months passed. By now, I was approaching my twenty-first birthday. I heard from Chris from time to time. He was learning to walk again, and he let me know he was also dating someone. So that door was not likely to open again.

Meantime, Nick would be home from his mission soon. I wrote to him, telling him of the past year and what had happened with Chris. Nick wrote back, and his letters were friendly but cool. His focus was still fully on his missionary work, and the sweet relationship we'd once had was no longer evident. Well, of course not.

When Nick got home, he seemed happy to see me. We dated once, but after that, he didn't call me or return any of my phone calls. I was deeply depressed, but I understood he really didn't trust me anymore after "Dear Johning" him.

It was summer again, and I had turned twenty-one. I was confused about my life. I prayed for direction. Should I give Nick more time to see if we could recapture what we'd once had? Or should I look for someone else? Or was it time to put in papers for a mission? Day after day, I received no witness or answer to my prayers. I needed to know whether or not to enroll for another semester at BYU, and since I didn't get an answer to serve a mission, I went ahead and enrolled.

Meantime, my parents had moved to Utah, and they invited me to live at home in Pleasant Grove, about a half-hour drive from BYU. Instead of attending a singles ward on campus, I attended one in the stake where my parents lived.

One afternoon, my mother received a phone call from a sister in her ward who asked if I could stop by on Sunday morning to pick up Beth, her granddaughter, and give her a ride to church. When Sunday arrived, I drove over to this sister's house and met Beth for the first time. She was tall, blonde, thin, and very pretty. We immediately became friends, and from that time on, we attended the singles ward and all of the activities together.

A few months later, on a fast Sunday, Beth went to the pulpit for the first time to share her testimony. She said she knew the Church was true, and then she invited everyone in the congregation to her baptism in two weeks! What a shock! We had all assumed she was a member of the Church—except for our bishop, who had kept her secret!

Beth shared with us that she had been quietly taking the missionary discussions, but she didn't want to tell anyone because she didn't want to be treated any differently. She wanted to see for herself what members of the Church were really like and if they really lived what they believed. She thanked all of us for our sincerity, love, and friendship, and the good spirit that she always felt at church.

The two weeks until her baptism passed quickly. I was still praying every day for direction. In fact, by then I had been praying for months, asking if the time was right for me to serve a mission, and I still had not received any answer. I was disheartened and began to doubt if I was ever going to be a missionary.

On the day of Beth's baptism, almost the entire singles ward attended. It was exciting to see Beth dressed in white and ready to enter the baptismal waters. She asked me to participate in her baptismal program, and I was pleased to help. I was so happy for her! The service began with the usual hymn and talk on baptism. Beth stepped down into the font and was baptized, and then she went back to the changing room.

While we waited for Beth to dress, the pianist began to softly play some hymns on the piano, and we all sat for a few moments of quiet reflection. I took this opportunity to ask Heavenly Father again, as I had so many times before, if I should serve a mission. Immediately, I felt as if heaven itself had opened up and the Spirit had poured into me. My heart began to burn, and my body tingled from head to toe. This feeling continued for several minutes, and there was absolutely no doubt in my mind that the time had finally come. I was to go on a mission! My joy was so incredible that I began to weep. I got a few odd stares from people sitting around me, but it didn't matter. I finally knew what course Heavenly Father wanted me to follow. With Beth's baptism, I had received my answer.

Within a few short weeks, my mission application was ready and sent off to Church headquarters. Before the end of the semester, I received my mission call to serve in the Honduras Tegucigalpa mission.

I entered the mission home in January 1995 and began one of the happiest, most fulfilling, and rewarding times of my life.

Eighteen months later, when I returned home and reported to the stake president about my mission, I sobbed when he asked me to take off my name tag because I was no longer a missionary. I had been honorably released. It was time to move forward to a new chapter in my life.

Looking back now, I believe the Lord led me to help others who needed me during the time I struggled to know whether or not to serve. Nick needed a friend. Chris needed a companion but not a wife at the time. And Beth needed a friend *and* a good example.

During that time leading up to my mission, I followed the promptings and impressions I received the best I knew how, even though I could not understand the path I was following very well. I see now the hand of the Lord in my life. I felt honored to be a servant of Jesus Christ and serve Him in some important ways, and I still feel that way to this day. I will never forget the powerful answer to serve a mission that I received at Beth's baptism. I felt a bit of heaven enter into me that day. It was an unforgettable witness of Heavenly Father's love for me. I know He guides our lives, even when we don't understand the path we are on very well.

Gina Lynn Shelley returned from her mission, graduated from BYU, and began attending the same singles ward as before. She met a returned missionary, Brian (her home teacher), and the two began dating and eventually married. She went on to earn her PhD from the University of Utah, and she currently works as an assistant professor at Ashford University in Clinton, Iowa. The Shelleys have four children. Besides parenting and teaching, Gina also enjoys scrapbooking, homemaking, performing arts, quilting, cooking, and traveling.

And whatsoever ye shall ask the Father in my name,
which is right, believing that ye shall receive,
behold it shall be given unto you.

—3 Nephi 18:20

Beyond My Ability

By Natalie Morton

I have read many books and magazine articles on parenting, both before and after I started my family. But nothing can really prepare you or help you more than real, personal, life experiences.

I had one of those moments several years ago when the Olympics came to Salt Lake City. We had seven children at the time. We were so excited to watch the Olympics as a family. We saw the runners come in with the torch, and then we went on to the University of Utah to witness the torch all lit up.

We would watch the different events on TV and even wander downtown to see and feel the excitement, watch all the people, and explore the different venues.

My husband, Dave, worked at the Triad Center, an office building in downtown Salt Lake City that faced the awards plaza. We were able to watch some of the awards ceremonies from his office. As the Olympics came to a close, we decided to take our seven children to the top of the Triad Center to watch the closing ceremony and fireworks. My husband and I met at a parking lot a couple miles away to join each other and drive downtown together. As we arrived, he got out of his car and I got out of our van, and we stood in the parking lot talking and formulating our plans. We worried about the crowds and traffic we would run into downtown.

When we got back into the van, we found chaos inside. Two of our children were crying and upset, and the others were shouting at each other. I finally found out that a fight had broken out between two of my boys. Then the older one had grabbed his younger brother with both hands and had tried to choke him! I could still see red marks around his neck.

I went into shock. I couldn't believe my two boys—boys we hoped would be close friends as they matured—would ever do such a thing. Still, I'd noticed that these two brothers had been struggling in their relationship for a while. I guess the tension had finally exploded, and one of them just snapped.

I also snapped. I began yelling threats myself. The first words out of my mouth were, "You are both grounded for a week. I HAVE HAD IT!"

Immediately, I knew I had to retract my words because I had just sentenced myself to coping with two boys being grounded for a week. But more importantly, I knew what I had just said was *not* the answer to helping my boys mend their relationship. It wasn't right.

I turned around and told them both I was upset and had overreacted. I would need to think about a punishment and would get back to them the following day.

All night as we watched the fireworks, I couldn't put out of my mind the fact that one of my sons had tried to choke another. It seemed so unreal. *How* could that happen? Where had I failed as a parent to have such a terrible thing happen? The fireworks ended late, and we finally drove home and put the kids to bed.

I had read an article in the *Ensign* several months earlier about two brothers who had begun to fight and a mother who had longed to repair their relationship. She had turned to the Lord for help and guidance. It was through prayer that she gained the answers to help them.

Of course. I didn't know how to fix this—or even if it could be fixed. My earthly knowledge, desires, capabilities, and good intentions as a parent weren't enough. I needed help beyond any ability I possessed.

That night, I knelt in prayer and asked Heavenly Father to help me know what I could do to handle this terrible behavior and my deep desire to help my sons so this would never happen again.

The next morning, knowing I couldn't put this off, I again prayed for help. As I knelt, pondering deeply, an idea came to mind. But in order to know how to best make it work, I would need the Spirit to be with me as I talked to my son. So much depended on my staying calm and following the impressions that had come to me. How I needed the Lord's help!

I rose from my prayers and invited my older son to chat with me. I began by talking to him about Heavenly Father's great plan for us to return to live with Him again and His great love for each one of us individually. I explained that He had created each one of us with great gifts and talents. We talked about those special gifts that were just my son's and what a great young man he was becoming.

Then I talked to him about what Heavenly Father might have thought as He created our legs for running, walking, and moving from place to place. He created our eyes to see those things we love and our ears to hear voices, laughter, and conversations. Finally, I asked, "What do you think He thought of when He created our hands?"

My son thought about that. He named several things: work, making things, serving others, giving a hug, and lovingly picking up younger brothers and sisters. Then we talked about Christ, who set a great example of what our hands should be used for. He blessed and healed the sick. He cared and loved others. He taught them in love and patience. And in the palms of His hands, He bore His greatest sign of love and sacrifice for us.

Then I proceeded to ask my dear son, "Do you think, in Heavenly Father's amazing plan to create our hands, that at anytime he thought they would be used to choke another person, hurt, or cause pain?" I suggested that every time he used his hands for good or ill, he might remember Heavenly Father's plan—what hands were created for and how the Savior's hands bore the sign of His sacrifice.

Finally, I talked to him about our hope as parents, to have all our sons enjoy a close and loving relationship, even to become best friends.

My son leaned over to me with huge tears in his eyes, and we cried together. He said he was sorry, and I sensed a strong connection between us. I knew Heavenly Father had heard the prayers of a desperate mother who needed guidance to know the *very best way* to help two sons who were acting out in unacceptable ways. And he had given me just the right words to touch *their* hearts.

Those two brothers never had another major blowup. It did take time and occasional reminders to turn their relationship around. But it did happen, and they eventually became best friends. To this day, they still enjoy spending time with each other. Now I see them joke and laugh together, and I feel such gratitude for my Heavenly Father, who knows who we are and the desires of our heart. He is there to help us as parents every step of the way.

Natalie Morton and her husband, Dave, live in Sandy, Utah, where Dave serves as a bishop. They are parents of ten children. Natalie enjoys family activities, such as swimming, kayaking, and riding four-wheelers with the children—and her Friday night dates with Dave!

Know ye not that ye are in the hands of God?

—Mormon 5:23

You'll Be All Right

By Janice LeFevre

One Friday evening in July 2001, our family was driving south from our home in northern Utah to Cedar City, Utah, where my husband's parents lived. We planned to stay there overnight and then drive on to California for a vacation with our cousins at the beach.

We'd driven less than halfway to Cedar City, with at least two and a half more hours to go, when the van's engine suddenly stopped. We coasted to the side of the road somewhere near Nowheresville, where there were no services. Vast stretches of high desert scenery stretched in nearly every direction. Across the valley, a few cultivated fields and farmhouses dotted the landscape—too far away for a quick walk for help. Immediately, our girls—Sarah, age nine, and Becca, age six—erupted with questions.

"Where are we?"

"Why're you stopping, Daddy?"

"Is someone carsick and needs air?"

"I think the van's broken," answered our oldest son, Josh, who spoke in his *I'm twelve years old, so I know more than you* voice.

"Yes, the van is broken," my husband, Steve, replied.

Worried, I looked over at him. We didn't own a cell phone, so we couldn't call for help, and sunset was just a couple hours away. Our only company was grasshoppers doing their hip-hop dance in the amber weed fields beside us and cars whooshing past us on the freeway.

"What do you think is wrong?" I asked.

"I don't know. Could be the alternator or the battery or a clogged fuel filter."

Steve got out of the van and looked under the hood, but he couldn't tell what was wrong. As he checked wires, hoses, and parts, I silently prayed that he would be able to figure out the problem and fix it. I also prayed for help to remain calm. Then I pasted on a smile and tried to keep the children happy.

"It's hot," Josh whined. "Turn on the air conditioner!"

"Sorry, but it won't work because the engine is broken." I opened all the doors so we could catch any breezes that might come.

"I'm hungry!" Becca said.

I gave the kids chewy granola bars, fruit snacks, and cups of water. Luckily, we were well stocked since I'd packed enough food for a two-day drive.

Meanwhile, Steve repeatedly tried to restart the engine. Nothing. He tried to wave down help from passing vehicles. No response. I looked toward the distant farmhouses and wondered if one of us should begin walking to one before dark. *Only if we have no other choice,* I decided. A couple years before, my cousin had been severely mauled by a large dog as he'd crossed a farmer's field to get help for his own family who'd been stranded in their crippled car. No matter that it was unlikely this tragedy would happen to me, I didn't want to risk repeating his experience.

As the minutes crept by, the kids' normal tussles and restlessness subsided. They became more somber.

"Will we have to sleep in the van?" Sarah asked, echoing my thoughts.

"I hope not," I said.

I checked the flashlight in the glove box. The bulb barely flickered as it drained the last of the battery. *Great,* I thought sarcastically. *We won't have a flashlight to help us if we have to stay here overnight or if we have to walk to a farmhouse for help.* I didn't relish crossing barbed-wire fences without a light.

Now increasingly worried, each child began asking questions about what we'd do if their dad couldn't fix the van.

"We don't know yet," I answered again and again as their queries ramped up my own anxiety. "Now, shh," I finally said, feeling a bit impatient. "I need you to play quietly. I need to think. Can you help us out that way?"

They nodded and began whispered hand games.

After a fruitless hour under the van's hood, Steve suggested we have family prayer. We bowed our heads while he asked the Lord to please fix our van long enough for us to get to Cedar City so we could have a safe place to spend the night and, we hoped, to find a good mechanic.

As Steve prayed, I felt a message play like a whisper through my thoughts: *The van will start. You will get to Cedar tonight, and you will be able to get to California on time. You'll be all right.* The Spirit seemed to blanket each of us with its assurance. As the prayer ended, I turned to the kids sitting in the backseats and told them what the Spirit had whispered. "Can you feel the special feeling in our van?" I asked.

They nodded, their expressions peaceful.

"What you are feeling is the Holy Ghost," I said. "Heavenly Father is helping us."

Steve turned the key in the ignition once again, and the van started immediately. The kids cheered and laughed. As we drove, I began to feel tense again as worries pushed into my mind, so I focused on God's promises and kept a prayer in my heart. My anxiety eased and then dissolved as I thanked the Lord for His blessings and expressed confidence in His continued help. We made it to Cedar City safely that night and without any more vehicle problems.

Once there, we discovered that if we wanted our van fixed in time to drive to California the next day, we'd have to go to an auto dealership in St. George, forty-five miles away, for repairs.

"I wonder if that's wise," Steve said as we counseled together. "I could be stranded again—there are no towns between here and there. Maybe we shouldn't be in such a hurry to get the van repaired. We could just stay the weekend with my parents and then see a mechanic here in Cedar City on Monday."

"I'm not sure what's best," I said. "I don't want to put you at risk, but at the same time, I think driving there will be okay because the inspiration we received earlier said we'd make it to California on time. The only way for that to happen is for you to go to St. George. We need to ask the Lord what to do."

Again, we prayed for guidance and help. The Lord blessed us with peace and assurance that He'd open the way and that Steve wouldn't get stranded. The next morning, he left early so he would arrive when the dealership opened, but when he got there, he learned the mechanics were completely booked.

As Steve telephoned me with this news, the shop manager tapped him on the shoulder and said, "We just had a cancellation for our next appointment. Would you like to take it?" The mechanics quickly diagnosed the problem as a broken fuel pump. It was in such bad shape that they were shocked Steve had been able to drive it to their shop.

By that afternoon, we were well on our way to California and had no further troubles.

The Lord, who usually works so quietly we must pay close attention in order to see His hand, provided a dramatic lesson about His love for and personal interest in us as He manifested His power in our behalf. This lesson is the greatest gift we received from this incident. In addition, Steve and I were given a powerful opportunity to teach our children—in a memorable way—how to rely on the Lord when troubles come.

Janice Stringham LeFevre is a mother of three and a historian, editor, freelance writer, and poet. Janice enjoys historical research, reading, traveling, playing games, and boogie boarding in the Pacific Ocean. She has served in various Church callings, including a full-time mission. Married to Steven Ronald LeFevre, she lives in Kaysville, Utah.

And if men come unto me I will show
unto them their weakness. I give unto men weakness
that they may be humble; and my grace is sufficient for
all men that humble themselves before me; for if they humble
themselves before me, and have faith in me, then will I
make weak things become strong unto them.

—Ether 12:27

Why Me?

By Shauna Dansie

I felt thrilled when, after sixteen years of marriage, we had a chance to move back to Salt Lake City, Utah. We had rambled all over the country—Arizona, Virginia, Nevada—loving every minute of new life experiences. Still, what a joy it was to have family nearby again and to return to the mountain-shadowed valley my soul longed to be near.

After serving in various auxiliary capacities for eleven straight years, I'll admit I welcomed an anticipated rest. With so many Church members in the state of Utah, I dreamed of a cushy, simple calling. I heard that people in large wards had callings like conducting Primary sharing time once a month. Indeed, within a week of our move, I received a call as a fourth-Sunday teacher in Relief Society. I had just been released from a three-year stint serving in a busy Relief Society presidency, so this calling to teach once a month would be a more manageable challenge. And that would be all! No more visits, meetings, or long Sundays.

But the Lord had different plans. Two weeks after accepting the call as a Relief Society instructor, I was once again called into the bishop's office. He asked if I would serve as the ward Relief Society president. He had tears in his eyes as he relayed a spiritual experience that made me believe he, at least, felt certain I belonged in that capacity. I said yes to the calling, more out of reaction and shock than a belief that I was fit to serve.

Me, president? Sure, I knew how to be a good supporter. But *president*? I could think of a hundred reasons why I was the least qualified. This was going to be a challenge—for a lot of reasons.

For one thing, I had never even graduated from seminary and had spent years in semi-activity. Since that time, though, I had served in many presidencies, but I had always comfortably worked in supporting roles. I had never before assumed the responsibility and carried the burden as ultimate decision maker. Certainly, I felt I was neither wise nor experienced enough to serve in this awesome capacity. Nor did I feel like I had the appropriate personality. I am a shy and private person. I prefer to work through life's challenges alone, so getting involved with other people's problems feels intrusive to me.

More importantly, perhaps, came a certain realization that the Lord fully understood my unique, individual characteristics. I had faced some difficult experiences, and I wondered if someone needed my compassion and understanding now. The Lord knew it was essential that I internalize an immediate lesson: *I would have to rely on the Spirit to guide me during every moment of my term as Relief Society president.*

Yet, I was nervous. Supporting a sister through difficult trials might require me to relive some very personal and private experiences. Would assisting someone else cause *me* to fall apart emotionally? I felt like there was no one to talk to about these concerns, and I experienced a great sense of insecurity. I had never realized before that leaders are surrounded by many people but often feel quite lonely.

However, as I grew in my calling, the support of the priesthood leaders I served with became an increasingly cherished gift that bridged that sense of isolation. The men in my ward reminded me of the meaning of priesthood power and the nobleness of truly righteous men.

During this season of service, I dealt with all the usual challenges facing most Relief Society presidents, including a few unusual ones. Dinners were taken in, service given, hurt feelings soothed. Sisters were called and released. Activities got organized, programs planned, and visiting teaching encouraged. During all of it, I watched and waited for that sister who needed something special, something only I could help with.

Three years and many experiences later, I was released as Relief Society president. It had turned out to be one of the most deeply meaningful experiences of my life. However, my release sent me into a period of personal questioning once again. Everything felt wrong. I had never helped another member in our ward through the trials I had anticipated. The purpose of my service, as I imagined it, had never come to fruition. In fact, I felt as if I hadn't really helped anyone in any particular way.

After many prayers, fasting, tears, and a bit of time and clarity, I came to realize that perhaps I was placed in the calling of Relief Society president because *I* was the sister who needed help. After all, didn't I have some issues in my heart and soul that I needed assistance to heal? I mentally reviewed the past three years and watched as the Lord had sent people to love, teach, and encourage me.

Father in Heaven knows me as an individual and loves me enough not only to show me my weaknesses but also to provide a journey wherein I could become stronger in those areas. In serving among the sisters of my ward, I was the one who grew, who experienced loving kindness, and whose faith deepened. I am honored that I was given this growth experience in my life.

I'm so grateful for the abundant tender mercies of the Lord, among them this calling. It taught me, among other things, not to spend so much time questioning and overthinking things I don't understand. But most of all, through it I found His influence had touched my heart and given me a gift of healing that has strengthened and sustained me ever since.

Shauna Dansie lives in South Jordan, Utah, with her husband, two daughters, and two cats named after candy bars. She is a multi-award-winning author who enjoys teaming with individuals and companies to help them create and communicate through writing. Shauna can be reached at shaunadansie@q.com.

Be of good comfort: thy faith
hath made thee whole; go in peace.

—Luke 8:48

The Answer Is No

Name Withheld

Some time ago I had an experience that can only be defined as a combination of *indescribable* and *unforgettable.* I was in my mid-twenties and had been married for four or five years—years of being on a disastrous emotional rollercoaster because of my apparent inability to become pregnant. After three years of ongoing, soaring hope that a pregnancy was finally in progress, only to be dashed by the realization that, once again, it wasn't true, I had finally decided, after exhausting all other options, to ask for a priesthood blessing.

The stake president agreed to fast with me for three days and then administer a blessing. (Church officials in Salt Lake City later announced that fasts of that length were completely unnecessary and that a more normal fast of twenty-four hours was sufficient.) After the blessing, I immediately became pregnant and was filled with incredible joy. We had our first child, a most beloved son.

Slowly, I realized the blessing didn't carry over for subsequent pregnancies. One, two, three years again went by with the same rollercoaster emotions that made life difficult for all of us, and I again decided I needed a priesthood blessing. Again, we fasted and prayed, and again, I was given a blessing. But to my surprise, there was no immediate pregnancy like there had been the first time.

It only took two or three months of waiting for this second miracle-that-never-happened for me to reach the end of my emotional resources. I couldn't understand why heaven was bypassing me, especially when it was obvious that other families, some of them far less worthy—so I thought at the time—were being blessed with large families. What was I missing here?

One evening at bedtime, I was emotionally exhausted. In a great state of turmoil, I flung myself to the floor by my bedside with the intention of getting some clear-cut, understandable answers to the prayers I was continuously offering. The agony of so much continued rejection and despair had piled up inside me until it had become an intolerable burden. I can't say I was suicidal, but I really couldn't see how I could go on living. I just wanted to *know* the will of the Lord so I could settle down with whatever realities were actually governing my existence.

I was so tired of waiting for what was always out of reach, hoping for another baby, only to have those hopes dashed on the rocks of cruel reality. What could be wrong? I always wondered. Why was the Lord constantly bypassing me? Was I evil in some way? Disobedient? Just stupid? Did the Lord think I could only handle one baby in my life? Hope and despair, hope and despair—these made a mishmash of my emotions and drained my strength.

I put it all straight to the Lord that night in two short sentences filled with so much emotion I could hardly get them out: *Am I going to have another baby or not? I just want to KNOW!* After that short prayer poured out of me, rude as it may seem, I immediately heard a very quiet, yet quite distinct voice say, "The answer is no." Before I could react, I was immediately flooded with the most wonderful, intense love. It was indescribable. I was *filled*. Every tiny area of my entire being was flooded with the sweetest, most inexpressible love. It was, indeed, sweeter than anything else on earth.

I had never experienced nor read of love such as this, and I was overwhelmed by its purity and power. The power that came upon me and filled me created a deep, overwhelming peace within my entire being. In addition, I felt as though a force field had been created around me so nothing could penetrate its shielding powers.

That love stayed with me for the next several days—I carried it with me everywhere I went, and I marveled that nobody sensed what I was experiencing or stopped to stare at me. I seemed to be a completely changed person.

I couldn't remember exactly what my problems had been—that is what was so amazing. When I finally "came to" and things began to normalize a few days later, I realized for the first time that what I had wanted didn't make a difference anymore—it *really* didn't matter. This love of the Lord was all I needed to balance and complete my life. I knew I could go forward with confidence that joy and fulfillment were possible for me, even though my life would apparently be different from what I had always imagined. For years after that experience, every time I asked the Lord if He still loved me, a similar but lesser manifestation was given me, so I always knew things were okay, no matter what those "things" were.

Later on, after the blessing, my husband and I applied for adoption. Four months later, a beautiful baby girl was placed in my arms, to be mine to love and cherish. Then, in incredible wonder, I realized about a week later that I was also *four months pregnant*—I had been pregnant when I had prayed! And the answer *no*, which I had assumed meant I would never have another child, meant instead that after I gave birth to *one more* child, I would have no more. I was suddenly overwhelmed at the Lord's bounty. I gave birth to our daughter and had two babies to care for. My cup truly was full.

In retrospect, I only realized years later what one possible reason was for why there would be no more babies coming to our family. This beautiful baby my husband and I had adopted turned out to have a number of special needs that often completely overwhelmed me—needs that continue on to this day, more than forty years later. I realize now that had I known immediately that I was pregnant with a second baby, I would never have applied for adoption. It seemed to me then, as it does now, that the Lord had desired that I be a mother to this oh-so-needy infant, and what better way could there have been to make the adoption happen?

I am often amazed at the way things have worked out through the wisdom of the Lord, and I can only praise Him and His very great intelligence and loving concern for someone such as myself. How can I ever complain? I can only praise the Lord and seek to do His will, knowing that, really, all is well.

And when ye shall receive these things, I would exhort you
that ye would ask God, the Eternal Father, in the name of Christ,
if these things are not true; and if ye shall ask with a sincere heart, with
real intent, having faith in Christ, he will manifest the truth of
it unto you, by the power of the Holy Ghost.
And by the power of the Holy Ghost ye may know
the truth of all things.

—Moroni 10:4–5

My Second Witness

By LaDeana Wilke

During my growing-up years in Salt Lake City, neither of my parents was an active member of the Church. I decided to attend seminary in the ninth grade because my friends wanted to go. My parents didn't care whether I went or not. At that time, ninth-grade seminary was held before school. I don't remember many of the Book of Mormon lessons Brother Grant, our teacher, taught us. However, I do remember feeling that he cared about his students and knew the Book of Mormon was true. At the beginning of the year, he encouraged us to read the Book of Mormon twice that year.

In January, I had finished reading it for the first time. As Moroni encouraged readers in Moroni 10:4–5, I knelt on the top bunk of my bunk bed to ask if this book was from God. I did not feel or hear anything as I waited patiently for an answer. Finally, tiredness overtook me, and I fell fast asleep. Sometime in the middle of the night, I sat up in bed and said to myself, "The Book of Mormon is the word of God—I know it is." I don't know what prompted that thought or why I felt that way, but I did feel it.

The next day, at the beginning of our seminary class, Brother Grant did something he had never done before and would never do again. He stood in the front of the class and said, "I bet I can name everyone in this classroom who has prayed about the truthfulness of the Book of Mormon and received an answer."

He then walked around the room, standing for a few moments in front of each student's desk. He never said anything until he came to the last desk, which was mine. Then he looked me in the eye and said, "You have."

Tears rolled down my face as I felt a warmth in my chest testifying that the witness I had received the night before was true and that the Book of Mormon was from God. I am so grateful for that second witness I received that morning from a caring seminary teacher. As I have pondered this incident many times, I have realized I needed another witness to help strengthen my understanding of the Spirit. Since I had not been taught the gospel in my home and did not know what a testimony was, this experience taught me how to recognize and trust the Spirit.

LaDeana Wilke lives in Liberty Township, Ohio, with her husband, Don. They have four grown children and one grandchild. LaDeana loves to write, garden, and create as much excitement in her household as possible. She also enjoys traveling with her husband now that most of their children have "flown the coop."

Be thou humble; and the Lord thy God shall
lead thee by the hand, and give thee answer to thy prayers.

—D&C 112:10

Back-Road Washout

By Patricia Thelin

Our family had been camping high in the mountains in northern Washington. It was time to go home, so I packed the van (a twelve-passenger van) with all the kids (six of mine, plus a few friends) and all the camping gear. As I left the campsite, I decided to have an adventure. I consulted a map and found a twisty dirt back road that wound its way through the mountains and eventually came out onto the main highway.

When we got to the turnoff, we looked at the dirt road. It looked okay, so we started on our way, bouncing along, enjoying our little adventure, and seeing some of the back-country sights. Gradually, the road became rougher, with many winding curves. The very size of the van made it increasingly difficult to maneuver. I began looking for a turnout or someplace to turn around. But the road was very narrow, and turning a long van around was impossible.

We kept going, threading our way through trees and mountain curves. Then, suddenly, we came to a place where the road had washed out along a steep mountainside. There was very little of it left—only enough space for the passenger side wheels to cross over. The mountain on one side was very steep, and the other side dropped off into a steep ravine.

The road had been twisting and turning along this steep mountainside for some time, and there was simply no place to turn around. Backing up for miles was out of the question. We couldn't very well sit there for the rest of our lives, but we were miles from civilization and it was highly unlikely that any cars would be coming by to help. We really could think of no other choice besides to go on. I would have to try to drive across the washed-out portion, even though one side of the van would be tilted on a steep mountainside.

I studied the steep hillside ahead. It seemed impossible that we wouldn't roll over. The van was simply too big to crawl across that wash-out safely. But I didn't know what else to do. I turned around and explained the situation to the children.

Then we prayed. We all folded our arms and prayed fervently that Heavenly Father would protect us. I instructed all the children to gather to the side of the van by the mountain to add more weight to that side. Very gingerly, I stepped on the gas and crept forward along the road with only two wheels on the narrow ledge. The van tilted precariously, and the children had to hang on tightly to stay glued to the left-side windows. My heart was hammering, and I continued to pray in my heart that I could get our family across this dangerous stretch and make it home safely. We slowly made it across without rolling over. As I steered back onto the graded road once more, relief washed over me.

We stopped the van, bowed our heads, and offered a prayer of thanksgiving. We eventually made it safely back to the main highway and home with very thankful hearts for Heavenly Father, who knows and loves us and rescues us from crazy situations we sometimes inadvertently get ourselves into!

Patricia Thelin lives in Bountiful, Utah. She loves to read, crochet afghans, go camping, solve logic problems, and play games, especially with her children and grandchildren.

Six days shalt thou labour, and do all thy work: But the seventh day is the sabbath of the Lord thy God . . . wherefore the Lord blessed the sabbath day, and hallowed it.

—Exodus 20:9–11

Noodles and Stroganoff

By Marci Thueson

Since we've often had company for Sunday dinner, keeping the commandment of not going to the store on Sundays was not always easy for me. However, the last few years I have really tried to keep that commandment. To do this, I have begun preparations for Sunday dinner on Saturday night by going grocery shopping. One Sunday, however, I really faced a challenge to my resolve.

Winter 2010 was hard on us. We were in the construction business, and the economy had been bad for our industry. Thus, we had very little income, and I had to save most of my food money for Sunday dinners. On this particular weekend, I was really tired after working all day, and since we were not expecting any company on Sunday, I decided to skip the trip to the store. We would make a meal for my husband, Kevin, and me and our two sons from whatever was in our fridge and freezer.

I was busy finalizing my lesson early Sunday morning, and just before I left for church, I looked in the freezer and found three little beefsteaks. Hardly enough for a family of four, but I thought I could make beef stroganoff and noodles, so they would do. I threw the small pieces of meat into the Crock Pot to simmer. I checked the cupboard for noodles but only found half a bag. Hmm. I checked the freezer and found some very old Rhodes roll dough that had probably been there for about three months. I didn't think the rolls would raise much, but even if they didn't, we could pretend they were biscuits. I laid them out on a cookie sheet and went to church.

After sacrament meeting, my husband and I were talking to a young man we had fellowshipped and who had recently been baptized. During the conversation, my husband just blurted out, "Why don't you come to dinner and bring your two friends along with you?" They gladly accepted and said they would be over a couple of hours after church let out.

This put me into a panic. I was frustrated with my husband and explained to him our sad dinner situation. He then offered to go to the store. It was very apparent that we didn't have enough to feed our company of three large men, my husband, my two sons, and me.

However, it was Sunday, and I had been trying so hard to keep the Sabbath day holy. Trying to set a good example, I told him not to go. We rushed home and looked in the crockpot. The steaks had shrunk. Then we looked at the flat rolls and half package of noodles and got a bit discouraged. My husband again offered to go to the store.

This is when I knew I needed help. I said, "Wait a minute."

I went to my room, knelt by the side of my bed, and turned to the Lord. I prayed that we would have enough for our friends and that we would all be fed so we could keep the Sabbath day holy.

After a couple minutes of pondering, I felt okay about everything, and my anxiety left me. I went back to the kitchen and told my husband I had said a prayer and that we needed to have faith that everything would be all right. We would make do with what we had.

My husband took the steaks out of the crockpot and started cutting the tender meat into small pieces. But the small pieces didn't stay in little squares. The meat shredded with every cut, and the more he cut, the more it fluffed up. To our amazement, the meat pile looked like it was growing. He even said, "Wow! This really made a lot more than I thought it would!"

I had made a lot of sauce to make up for the lack of meat, but when we put the meat in, we found a perfect ratio of meat to sauce, and the large crockpot was overflowing!

I then turned and looked at the sad amount of noodles floating in the water. I knew we wouldn't have enough for everyone. I drained the noodles, but as I poured the water out, I noticed a large amount of noodles in the strainer. Confused, I tried to put them back in the pot, and they *would not fit*. I had to get another extra-large bowl to put them in!

About this time, our friends showed up.

"Wow, are you cooking noodles for the whole southern hemisphere?" one of the guys walking through the door said.

It was truly an amazing comment when I'd only had a less-than-half-full bag to start with. There were so many noodles!

A loud beep came from the oven. Our pathetic rolls were finished. I opened the oven door, and to my surprise, they were not pathetic anymore. Somehow they had risen to become beautiful, fluffy rolls. I was in complete shock. I had let the rolls raise for at least seven hours, and they had still been flat when I'd put them in the oven.

We sat down to enjoy our meal. We thanked our Lord for this wonderful blessing! When we finished serving, we found plenty left for seconds. Then, later, as our friends got ready to leave, we realized we still had stroganoff and noodles to spare. Since they were bachelors, our three friends took home some leftovers for their dinner the next night.

Every Sunday I try to take dinner to my neighbor next door, so I checked the pans, and I still had enough to share. I filled a plate and sent it next door. That evening, a Korean couple with three teenage boys showed up unexpectedly. New in our country, they were struggling with money. But aside from that, they were always curious and interested in what Americans eat. We had enough to feed them all and even enough to send some food home with them! Finally, late that night as I was putting away the leftovers, I realized we even had enough for dinner the next day for our family!

I don't know how it happened. I not only learned a powerful lesson about keeping the Sabbath day holy and relying on the Lord, but I also learned that the Lord always makes a way for you to help others. He will bless you abundantly . . . even if it is with noodles.

My children call this the story of the noodles and stroganoff, instead of the story of the loaves and the fishes.

I know the Lord is there for us when we choose to do right. He showed me that day that He truly wanted me to keep the Sabbath day holy.

Marci and her husband, Kevin, live in Bountiful, Utah. They have four awesome children—two married and two still at home—and one grandson. Besides helping run a family business, Marci serves on the stake Young Women board. When she has the time, she loves to garden, scrapbook, travel, hang out with her children, and do missionary work.

About the Author

Judy C. Olsen has been writing and editing for many years. She has published several books, both fiction and nonfiction, as well as many magazine articles and short stories. As a former editor for the *Ensign* magazine, Judy loves writing about people who live the gospel. She and her husband, Donald, live in Sandy, Utah, and have four children and sixteen grandchildren.

I wish to thank those readers of volume 1 who submitted stories to this work, volume 2. Without their contributions, we would not share in the bounty of spiritual insights this book offers.

If you feel you have a story that might strengthen others and build testimonies and wish to share it, please contact me at judyedits@gmail.com.

You can visit my website at www.olseneditorial.com.